970.498
V3665 VanStone
        Eskimos of the Nushagak
        River
                        80306

DATE DUE

NOV 20 1986	MAY 26'93	DEC 12 '97	
DEC 1987 3	SEP 30'98	NOV 30 '98	
No 15'90	NOV 17'93	JUL 22 '99	
5-30-91	FEB 10'94	JUL 28 99	
Ju 25'92	MAR 24'94		
Se 24'92	JUN 23'94	OCT 16 '00 JAN 31 '01	
OCT 01 1992			
Oc 29'92	NOV 03'94	DEC 02 02	
D 10'92	DEC 01'94	SEP 30 2018	
Ma 18'93	APR 13 1995		
Ap 15'93	SEP 30'97 OCT 14 97		

UNIVERSITY OF WASHINGTON PUBLICATIONS IN ANTHROPOLOGY

VOLUME 15

ESKIMOS OF THE NUSHAGAK RIVER

◆◆◆

AN ETHNOGRAPHIC HISTORY

by James W. VanStone

UNIVERSITY OF WASHINGTON PRESS
Seattle and London

IN MEMORY OF J. L. GIDDINGS

Preface

◆◇◆

THIS IS AN ACCOUNT OF HUMAN POPULATIONS IN THE NUSHAGAK
River region of southwestern Alaska through an application of the
research methods of history and anthropology. Of the two methods, history has ben used more extensively, but the historical
data are at all times subjected to ethnological interpretations. The
result is, then, a study in culture history and it points up a
significant fact about the nature of ethnographic studies in southwestern Alaska and in many other parts of the world as well: the
type of ethnographic field work carried out in the past is not possible today. A picture of the aboriginal culture or the early period
of contact with Europeans may not be adequately reconstructed
through work with informants alone. Even in a comparatively isolated area such as the one under discussion, where aboriginal life
ways have persisted for a long period of time compared to other
areas of North America, few informants are to be found who recall even the period when the impact of an alien culture was relatively restricted. The best that can be hoped for is that historical-
ly minded individuals will preserve information obtained from
older relatives and that they will be able and interested enough
to pass the information along at second or third hand to the eth-
nographer.

The absence of skilled informants does not mean, however, that
the past is dead. There are other methods of obtaining ethnographic data. In the Nushagak River region the period of historic
contact dates from the beginning of the nineteenth century, and
abundant documentary information exists on most phases of the
early relations between Europeans and the Eskimos they found in

the area. In addition, the techniques of archaeology may, in this case, be viewed as an extension of historical research and standard ethnographic field methods. Even without actual excavation, much can be learned about settlement patterns, about number and spatial arrangement of dwellings and other structures, ecological setting, spatial arrangement of village sites in relationship to one another, etc.

But this book is not a traditional ethnography; its purpose is not to present a reconstruction of aboriginal life in the Nushagak River region. It is a study in culture change, an examination of an Eskimo culture under the impact of increasing contact with and pressure from the outside world. Simply stated, my objectives have been as follows: first, to outline the history of Russian and American exploration of the Nushagak River, its major tributaries, and the adjacent region of Bristol Bay; second, to record the activities of the various agents of change in the Nushagak River region throughout the period of historic contact; third, to reconstruct population groupings, settlement patterns, and the yearly cycle of subsistence activities in the nineteenth century; and fourth, to describe contemporary subsistence activities and the present-day settlement pattern.

Of necessity, the material to be presented here consists, for the most part, of a straightforward historical narrative. No strong theoretical point of view runs through this study yet, hopefully, some form of historical pattern emerges that is meaningful beyond the immediate area and circumstances described. Hopefully, too, the changing life ways of the inhabitants of the Nushagak River region will be understandable in terms of what we know about relations between Eskimos and Europeans in other parts of Alaska.

The research methods on which this study is based are basic to more sophisticated anthropological studies and interpretations of the area. Given the impossibility of reconstructing an aboriginal baseline against which to measure the Nushagak River culture of today, it would seem that the next best thing is to provide a documented study of early aspects of change which, incomplete as this must necessarily be, nevertheless provides the vitally important background that makes the present understandable. Therefore the data and interpretations that follow should be regarded as a background study serving to call attention to an important and hitherto neglected area of Alaska, and at the same time suggesting future lines of research among the contemporary inhabitants.

Acknowledgments

THE FIELD WORK ON WHICH THIS STUDY IS BASED WAS FINANCED IN 1964 by the University of Toronto and the National Museum of Canada and in 1965 by the latter institution. I am grateful to Drs. A. D. DeBlois and David J. Damas, Human History Branch, National Museum of Canada, for their assistance and encouragement.

In the field the following individuals were particularly helpful in contributing time and effort toward the assemblage of the historical and ethnographic data in this study: Mr. and Mrs. C. J. Stovall, Mr. and Mrs. Alfred Andree, Mrs. H. P. Nicholson, Mr. and Mrs. Donald Sagmoen, Mr. and Mrs. Joe McGill, Mr. John Nelson, Mr. Peter Nelson, and Mr. Charles Franklin, all of Dillingham; Mr. Antoine Johnson, Mr. Charles Nelson, Mr. Ivan Ishnook, and Mr. Blunka Ishnook of Koliganek; Mr. and Mrs. John Dull, Jr., of New Stuyahok, and Mr. Paul Romie of Ekwok. I also wish to thank Mr. Elmer L. Smith, Deputy Magistrate at Dillingham, for allowing me to examine vital statistics records in his office and for much useful and valuable information on the Seventh Day Adventist colony on Lake Alegnagik. Father Vsevolod Rochcau, formerly of Dillingham, took an active interest in the research and, at a considerable sacrifice of his own time, helped me to make valuable contacts in Dillingham. Without his assistance, much of the field data basic to this study could not have been obtained in the time available.

For assistance in obtaining much of the historical material on which this study is based, I wish to express appreciation to the reference staff of the University of Toronto Library, to Mr. Edward L. Keithahn, formerly Curator, and Mrs. Phyllis Nottingham, Librarian, of the Alaska Historical Library and Museum in Juneau, Mr. Henry L. Williams, Harvey Memorial Library, Moravian College, Bethlehem, Pennsylvania, and to Mr. Vernon Nelson, Archivist, Archives of the Moravian Church, Bethlehem. Information on the Nushagak River region in the Russian-American Company Records, deposited in the National Archives and available on seventy-seven microfilm reels, was extracted and translated for me by Mr. Winston Sarafian of the University of California, Los Angeles.

For critical comments and useful suggestions during the preparation of this book I am grateful to Dr. Joan B. Townsend of the University of Manitoba. Appreciation is also due to Dr. Wendell H. Oswalt of the University of California, Los Angeles, who first called my attention to the Nushagak River region as a promising area for combined historical and ethnographic research. Dr. Oswalt also read the first two drafts of this study and was helpful in the development of its present organization.

NOTE ON TRANSLITERATION AND DATES

Russian words have been transliterated according to a modified form of the Library of Congress system except where translations have been used, in which case the original transliterations have been retained. All dates prior to 1867 are according to the Georgian calendar, which was twelve days behind the Julian calendar in the nineteenth century

JAMES W. VANSTONE

Chicago, Illinois
May, 1967

Contents

◇◆◇

Maps

———————————————————————————————
◈◈◈
———————————————————————————————

Introduction: Geographical and Ethnographical Background

A GEOLOGIST WHO TRAVELED EXTENSIVELY IN THE NUSHAGAK RIVER region in the 1930's divided the area into three geographic units (see map 3). These are: the lowland region of the Nushagak River and Bay, the Nushagak Hills, and the Tikchik Mountains (Mertie, 1938, p. 9). The Nushagak River, the main topographic feature of the entire region, rises in the Nushagak Hills and flows in a generally southward direction until it reaches tidewater at the head of Nushagak Bay. A tributary of the Nushagak, the Nuyakuk River, drains the six northern lakes that comprise part of the Tikchik Mountains geographical unit—the Tikchik Lakes. The four lakes immediately to the south and also part of this unit are drained by the Wood River which flows into Nushagak Bay; they are called the Wood River Lakes.

●Beginning with the lowland region of the Nushagak River and Bay, this unit may be divided into two sections: the flat, almost treeless area around Nushagak and Kvichak bays, and the alluvial flats of the Nushagak River. For the pusposes of this study, the mouth of the Nushagak River is considered to lie just south of the Wood River mouth, on a line between Dillingham and Picnic Point● The seaward region is regarded as Nushagak Bay. Only at Black Point, about twenty miles to the southeast of Dillingham, does the river begin to maintain a continuous downstream current, while the effect of the tides is present as far upstream as Portage Creek. In the same manner, on the Wood River the tides are occasionally noticeable throughout the entire length of the river to its source at the lower end of Lake Aleknagik. Mertie reports (1938, p. 10) that during very high tides the normal current out of the lake may actually be reversed; at these times the water level at the lower end of the lake may be raised as much as eight inches. These effects are, according to Mertie, owing to the fact that the tidal waters, although they reach a maximum of only nineteen feet at Clark's Point and twenty-one feet at Dillingham, pile up in the lower regions of the Wood and Nushagak rivers and thus raise the water upstream several feet. In the case of the Wood River, however, the effects of the tide are rarely noticeable much beyond the mouth of the Muklung River.

Nushagak Bay is a large tidal embayment about twenty miles wide at the point where it opens into Bristol Bay. The bay is funnel-shaped and narrows to about two and one-half miles off Dillingham at the mouth of the Nushagak River. From Etolin Point northward there are many shifting channels and shoals in the middle of the bay with extensive tidal flats and shoals along the west side as far as Coffee Point. The ship channel seems to vary, but generally lies west of the center of the bay, and ranges in depth from eight fathoms off Coffee Point to about four fathoms off Dillingham. The tidal currents are said to be strong, with the ebb being slightly stronger because of the current from the Nushagak and Wood rivers.

•The country bordering on Nushagak Bay is, for the most part, a swampy lowland, virtually treeless and possessing a tundra type of vegetation• Along the beach are gray silts that form the tidal flats. The beach is gravelly in some places, particularly where the land rises to form cliffs of alluvial material. On the west side of the bay and northeast of the Snake River, the land is low and tundra covered in some places, but rises occasionally to form bluffs sixty to one hundred feet in height. In the region around Dillingham stands of spruce begin to appear and continue northward as isolated patches to the Wood River Lakes. On the east side of Nushagak Bay the foreland rises in gently rolling benches to a height of more than two hundred feet in the vicinity of the Nushagak village site. The coast south of this point consists either of gravelly bluffs or moderate slopes well back from the water with a silt plain in front of them along the shore.

The vast valley lowland of the Nushagak River spreads about

ninety miles to the north and is about sixty miles wide from the eastern extremities of the Tikchik Mountains to the Kvichak River. The Nushagak River estuary, which spreads from Black Point to the mouth of the Wood River and runs in a northwesterly direction, has a length of about twenty miles and an average width of two miles. Dark gray mud flats border both sides of this estuary. On the northwest bank the lowland is higher and alder brush fringes the shore. The flats along the southwest bank, however, rise only slightly above the level of high tide and are covered with a thick growth of marsh grass. These low flats spread to the south for a distance of approximately two miles but wedge out toward Black Point. Beyond the mud flats in a southerly direction toward the bay are treeless plains of gravel, sand, and clay ranging from one hundred to two hundred and fifty feet in elevation and dotted with small lakes.

Above Black Point the Nushagak River is a moderately swift, shallow stream which is frequently braided with sloughs and channels, ranging from very short to ten miles in length. From a point about ten miles east of Black Point and continuing upstream for about twenty miles the Nushagak is divided into two large channels of approximately equal size. The eastern channel is known as the Keefer Cutoff; the western channel is the one used by all river traffic. Above the split the river is more or less confined to one channel although, as previously mentioned, there are many sloughs, islands, and gravel bars. The river is navigable for small boats well north of the boundary of this study and during the summer of 1964, heavily loaded barges made their way up the river nearly as far as the mouth of the Nuyakuk River with materials for the construction of a school at New Koliganek.

The west bank of the Nushagak River from the mouth of the Iowithla River upstream to a point approximately ten miles above the mouth of the Mulchatna River is bordered by a steep bluff that ranges from forty to two hundred feet above the level of the river. This bluff is the eastern edge of a great undulating plain composed of gravel, sand, and clay that forms the topography of the vast stretch of country between the Nushagak River and the Tikchik Mountains. This plain is covered with moss, grass, and brush, but along the river, beginning just above Black Point, stands a strip of timber that continues upstream into the

Nushagak Hills, growing thinner above the mouth of the Mulchatna and again above the mouth of the Nuyakuk River. This
timber consists mainly of spruce and poplar with some birch in
the better drained areas along the west bank. Two important
landmarks in this plain between the Nushagak River and the
mountains are the Muklung Hills and Kemuk Mountain, two
groups of low, rounded hills that rise above the plain. The Muklung Hills have an elevation of 2,800 feet, while Kemuk Mountain
is about 1,000 feet lower. The Kokwok River, the most important
tributary of the Nushagak along its west bank below the mouth
of the Nuyakuk, drains most of the area between the Muklung
Hills and Kemuk Mountain.

The east bank of the Nushagak River from Portage Creek
northward to a point opposite the mouth of the Nuyakuk is much
lower than the west bank and rises no more than five to twenty
feet above the water level. The first well defined bluffs on this
side of the river occur about four miles above the mouth of the
Mulchatna, the largest eastern tributary of the Nushagak. The
Mulchatna is timbered along its course in much the same manner
as the Nushagak; and the vast, low plain of this important tributary is an undrained country covered with hundreds of small
lakes. The Mulchatna has headwaters in the southern foothills of
the Alaska Range which border Iliamna Lake (see map 2). The
heaviest timber in the Nushagak drainage basin stands in the
lower part of the Mulchatna valley.

About five miles east of the confluence of the Nuyakuk and
Nushagak rivers, a low, rounded mountain rises approximately
1,600 feet above the surrounding plain. This prominent landmark,
known as Ketok Mountain, marks the southern end of the divide
that separates the drainage basins of the Mulchatna and upper
Nushagak rivers.

The Nuyakuk River is the principal western tributary of the
Nushagak. It flows out of Tikchik Lake in an easterly direction
for about forty miles before joining the Nushagak. This beauti-
ful stream, with high banks on both sides, is clear and deep with
a moderate current. Just below Tikchik Lake is a short stretch of
fast water and about three and one-half miles below the lake is a
small waterfall. A third stretch of swift water occurs about six miles
below the lake. With one or two exceptions, the country close to

the river exhibits little relief. The riverbanks are well wooded with spruce, poplar, and willow.

The Tikchik Mountains, as Mertie uses the term, constitute the eastern part of an extensive range known as the Kuskokwim Mountains, the southern limit of which is about twenty miles north of the head of Nushagak Bay (see map 2). Since these mountains, designated Wood River Mountains on United States Geological Survey quadrangle maps, are, for the most part, outside the area of this study, little will be said about them except to note that in the interlake area the peaks are less abrupt than further to the west and their tops are either flat of rounded in outline. At many places, these rounded hills occur as isolated buttes, or groups of several buttes, separated from one another by broad, low, alluviated valleys. The easternmost spurs of the hills project outward into the lowland of the Nushagak River. In the interlake area, the average height of these hills ranges from 1,500 to 2,500 feet. All the eastern front of the Tikchik Mountains drains into the twelve lakes, which in turn discharge into rivers that flow into Nushagak Bay.

The precipitation falling on the Nushagak River region, although light when compared with southeastern Alaska, is more than twice as great as that in the upper Yukon valley. About half the precipitation falls during the summer months, and summer weather generally is cool although there are a few warm days similar to those that characterize interior Alaska. The summer season is somewhat longer than in interior Alaska with frost being uncommon after June 1 and before September 1. The greatest extremes of temperature recorded at Dillingham and Nushagak from 1881 to 1919 were 80 and −54. During the summer of 1964, an exceptionally dry and warm season, temperatures were frequently in the high seventies particularly in late June and early July.

• The larger animals native to the Nushagak region are the moose, caribou, black bear, and brown bear, but none of these appear to be plentiful.• Moose are said to be scarce in the region of the Wood River Lakes, but are common around the Tikchik Lakes and along the Nushagak River. During air surveys in the summers of 1964 and 1965, moose appeared to be plentiful in the broad lowland extending west of the Nushagak River and along the Nuyakuk and Mulchatna rivers. Black and brown bears were also occasionally seen in these areas.

The more common smaller animals are the beaver, mink, lynx, fox, porcupine, land otter, and muskrat, but only the beaver, fox, and mink are of much importance as a source of commercial fur. Geese and ducks nest in the region and are seen at favored localities. On Nushagak Bay and along the larger rivers the arctic tern, jager, marsh hawk, kingfisher, and other birds may be seen. Rock and willow ptarmigan seem to be frequent visitors. The Tikchik and Wood River lakes afford ideal spawning grounds for the various varieties of salmon, and Bristol Bay and its arms have become the greatest red salmon fishing grounds in the world, a fact that has had a tremendous effect on the human population of the entire area. The lakes are also the habitat of Dolly Varden, rainbow, and lake trout. All these, together with whitefish, provide important sources of food for the Eskimos.

• The Eskimos of Alaska, from Greenland to northern Alaska, are noted for the uniformity of their speech. Equally noteworthy, however, is the linguistic break that occurs in the vicinity of Golovin on the north coast of Norton Sound, a boundary that represents a major cleavage within Eskimoan. The term *Inupik* is generally used to denote the northern and eastern language, while the term *Yupik* designates the southern division, that is, the western Eskimo language stock. This latter linguistic group has been separated by Hammerich (1958, pp. 632-639) into three major dialect clusters, *Yuk*, *Cux*, and *Sux*. Yuk is a mainland dialect that is limited distributionally to an area extending north to Golovin and south to Bristol Bay and the western end of Iliamna Lake. The inland range of Yuk is to the village of Paimiut on the Yukon River and the vicinity of Aniak on the Kuskokwim River. The Yuk-speaking Eskimos think of themselves as Yupik, or "real people," and some authors refer to the language by this designation. The Cux dialect is spoken only by the inhabitants of Nunivak Island, while Sux speakers are to be found in Prince William Sound, in the Kodiak-Afognak area, and along the south shore of the Alaska Peninsula.

The Nushagak River region lies well within the boundaries of the Yuk dialect and although there is linguistic uniformity, some ethnic diversity apparently existed at the time of first historic contact. Speaking generally, the Eskimos of Alaska are divided into small enclaves which are not tribes in the strict sense because they possess no tribal organization. They are, however, recognized entities representing varying kinds of ecological adaptation. The problem of accurately identifying the subcultural affiliation of those Eskimos in the Nushagak area is complicated because of conflicting statements made by nineteenth-century observers and, more particularly, because Eskimos from other areas have infiltrated the region from the time of the very earliest records right up until the present. This will be discussed in detail in Chapter VII. Here it is sufficient to note that a consensus of the sources makes a distinction between the coastal Eskimos of the Nushagak Bay area and those who lived along the river itself. The bay was inhabited by the Aglegmiut whose territory included most of the Alaska Peninsula to the southwest as far as Port Moller and to the northeast up to and including the western two-thirds of Iliamna Lake. The Nushagak River Eskimos have an ethnic name of Kiatagmiut. This subgroup of Yuk speakers occupied, at the time of historic contact, virtually the entire Nushagak River and the area to the west as far as and including the Wood River Lakes and the Tikchik Lakes.

These subcultural enclaves are somewhat different in population and size of the area occupied. The territory of the Aglegmiut covered 262 square miles and had an estimated population of 1,900 at the beginning of the historic period. It is probable, however, that no more than 500 of these lived around the shores of Nushagak Bay. The Kiatagmiut occupied 97 square miles with a population of approximately 400. The closest neighbors of the Aglegmiut were the Aleut to the southeast, the Kiatagmiut to the north, and the Tanaina Indians to the northeast. The Kiatagmiut shared common boundaries with the Togiagamiut of the Togiak River, the Kuskowagamiut of the Kuskokwim River, the Aglegmiut, and the Tanaina. Considering the diversity of the ethnic boundaries in southwestern Alaska, it is little wonder that these became blurred as a result of the fur trade, epidemics of introduced European diseases, the establishment of schools and missions, and particularly the emergence of an important commercial salmon fishery in Bristol Bay. Significantly, however, the Nushagak is the only river emptying into the Bering Sea that had a different ethnic group at its mouth than the one living along its interior banks and tributaries.

If one considers the major Eskimo subsistence pattern areas throughout Alaska, it can be noted that in the northern Inupik-speaking area the northwest coast of Seward Peninsula and the far northern coast between Point Hope and Point Barrow was occupied by the arctic whalers who subordinated all other subsistence activities to that specialized pursuit. South and east of these regions lived the arctic hunters and fishermen who carried out a diversified subsistence pattern based on sea mammal hunting, some caribou hunting, and fishing. In the interior or northwest Alaska lived the Nunamiut who were almost exclusively caribou hunters. Almost all the Yupik-speaking area of Alaska, with the exception of those regions to the extreme south where Suk was spoken, was inhabitated by Bering Sea hunters and fishermen whose subsistence pattern resembled that of their northern relatives except for a greater reliance on salmon fishing. The importance of this latter activity is emphasized by the fact that along the major rivers of southwestern Alaska—the Yukon, Kuskokwim, Togiak, Nushagak and Naknek—the Eskimos stressed salmon fishing above all other subsistence pursuits. The Suk-speaking area of Kodiak Island and Prince William Sound was inhabited by Pacific whalers and fishermen (Oswalt, 1967).

Turning our attention to a more detailed consideration of the Yuk area, we note that the cultural center of this dialect group was along the central Bering Sea coast. Here the people were oriented toward a maritime economy in which the seal was the most important animal killed. On the adjacent tundra there was some caribou hunting, and fishing for salmon was significant at the mouths of rivers and in certain bays. The Yuk penetration of the Nushagak River system, as well as of other river systems in southwestern Alaska, took place at some unknown time during the late prehistoric period when the people moved inland from the Bering Sea coast. It is not out of the question, however, that in the distant past, a caribou hunting population, with a culture similar to that found at early interior sites further to the north and also at several places on the Alaska Peninsula, may have occupied the upper Nushagak area. At any rate, the course of Eskimo prehistory in the area must be based mainly on speculation because the limited archaeological work has been carried out with reference only to sites of the historic period.

Two excavations are significant because of what they reveal about riverine Eskimo culture during the nineteenth century. The first of these took place at the central Kuskokwim River community of Crow Village (Oswalt and VanStone, 1967) and the second at Tikchik, a village near the mouth of the Tikchik River in the upper Nushagak River region (VanStone, n.d.). Both of these sites were occupied at least as early as 1820 and until the turn of the century. Artifacts suggest that the inhabitants possessed a cultural inventory that accurately reflected a segment of nineteenth-century coastal Bering Sea Eskimo material culture. The significant thing about these latter people, as we have already noted, is that they possessed a material culture that was not only well adapted to sea mammal hunting and trapping on land, but also to the taking of fish. They were thus able to adjust economically to any environmental situation that was compatible with their varied technology. So when these people entered the Kuskokwim and Nushagak river systems, fishing and land hunting methods were emphasized while the sea mammal hunting technology withered away and was forgotten.

At the same time, however, it seems that close ties were always maintained between the coastal Bering Sea peoples and those living along the major rivers. In this context it might be useful to conceive of a configuration of Alaskan riverine characteristics that is applicable throughout southwestern Alaska and in some northern areas as well. The traits would include diverse fishing techniques for taking several varieties of salmon and whitefish in particular. The use of trees is important and the relative stability of the physical settlement is a function of the productivity of the environment. Also of considerable importance is the trade with coastal Eskimos in which there is an exchange of riverine products for those of the sea coast. Like most Eskimos, these people maintained a flexibility in their subsistence pursuits. They exploited land animals as well as fish, but their economic stability came from fishing.

Although little is actually known concerning prehistory in the Nushagak River region, later chapters of this study will make plain that at the time of first historic contact the Kiatagmiut were exploiting effectively an inland environment and at the same time maintaining contact with the coastal Aglegmiut. This latter sub-cultural enclave can be thought of as representing the typical coastal Bering Sea Eskimo culture with its more generalized approach to the solution of subsistence problems. Even after more than a century of intensive and rapid cultural change, the basic attributes of both configurations remain important and valued aspects of Eskimo life in the area.

PART ONE: Agents of Change

I

Russian and American
Exploration, 1778-1935

◆◇◆

THE NUSHAGAK RIVER REGION AND THE BRISTOL BAY AREA, WHICH WAS
to be the locale of flourishing Russian mission and trading activity
between 1818 and the purchase of Alaska by the United States in
1867, was first visited and described by an Englishman. On July
9, 1778, Captain James Cook, on the third of his great voyages to
the Pacific Ocean, while working his way along the north coast of
the Alaska Peninsula in the *Resolution,* found himself in a great
bay that seemed to impede his progress to the north.

> The coast extended as far as North East half North, where it
> seemed to terminate in a point, beyond which we hoped and
> expected, that it would take a more Easterly direction. But soon
> after, we discovered low land, extending from behind this point,
> as far as North West by West, where it was lost in the horizon;
> and behind it was high land, that appeared in detached hills.

> Thus the fine prospect we had of getting to the North vanished in
> a moment. I stood on till nine o'clock, for so long it was light, and
> then the point above mentioned, bore North East half East, about
> three miles distant. Behind this point is a river, the entrance of
> which seemed to be a mile broad; but I can say nothing as to its
> depth. The water appeared discoloured, as upon shoals, but a calm
> would have given it the same aspect. It seemed to have a winding
> direction, through the great flat that lies between the chain of
> mountains to the South East, and the hills to the North West. It
> must abound with salmon, as we saw many leaping in the sea

3

before the entrance; and some were found in the maws of cod which we had caught. The entrance of this river, distinguished by the name of *Bristol River*, lies in the latitude of 58° 27′, and in the longitude of 201° 55′ (Cook and King, 1785, vol. II, pp. 428-429).

Captain Cook veered to the northwest toward Cape Newenham without landing in the Bristol Bay area. Although he never saw any part of the Nushagak or Kvichak rivers, he correctly postulated the existence of a river system at the head of Bristol Bay. His maps of the bay area are remarkably accurate.

The date of the first Russian penetration of the Nushagak River region cannot be determined with any degree of assurance. In 1791 Dmitri Ivanovich Bocharov, a naval officer acting under orders from the famous Alexander Andreevich Baranov (then associated with Grigori Ivanovich Shelikov as manager of the latter's company with headquarters on Kodiak Island), explored some of the northern part of the Alaska Peninsula, making efforts to establish friendly relations with the inhabitants in the interest of the fur trade. Bocharov may have reached Iliamna Lake and perhaps also the Nushagak River (Zagoskin, 1956, p. 421). During the struggles between the Shelikov and Lebedev-Lastochkin companies for control of the Cook Inlet area, members of the latter company, in 1792, are supposed to have plundered Iliamna and Nushagak villages that Bocharov had befriended (Bancroft, 1886, p. 340). Among the plunderers may have been Aleksei Ivanov who, sometime in the early 1790's, crossed from Cook Inlet to Iliamna Lake, descended the Kvichak to Bristol Bay and ascended the Nushagak. Ivanov then apparently crossed the mountains to the Holitna, descended that river to the Kuskokwim, and traveled downstream as far as the village of Ohogamiut where he may have portaged to the Yukon (Chernenko, 1956, p. 15; fn. 4, p. 15). Information concerning this journey is extremely scanty, but it seems to have been the first Russian penetration of the interior of southwestern Alaska.

In 1818, just before Baranov was replaced as general manager of the Russian-American Company, an expedition was dispatched by land to explore thoroughly the territory to the north of Bristol Bay. In November, 1817, Captain Leonti Andrianovich Hagemeister, who had been designated Baranov's successor by the directors of the company, arrived at Sitka with his assistant, a naval lieutenant named Semen Ivanovich Yanovski. The new administrators did not take up their duties until the following year and, according to Bancroft (1886, p. 522), Yanovski was a member of the expedition sent to the Bristol Bay area. He is not mentioned in Berkh's (1823) account of the exploration but he played an important part in subsequent decisions concerning the post established at the mouth of the Nushagak River by this expedition.

Although the 1818 expedition is said to have been ordered by the "general administration" (Tikhmenev, 1930-40, pt. 1, p. 300), Baranov himself was very likely responsible (Bancroft, 1886, p. 520). If this is so, the order must have been one of his last official acts. The party appears to have been under the direction of Petr Korsakovski (or Korsanovski, see Berkh, 1823, p. 46), an employe of the Russian-American Company who "had some knowledge of surveying and of trade relations with the natives who lived there" (Tikhmenev, 1939-40, pt. 1, p. 300). In addition to Korsakovski, the party also consisted of apprentice navigator Andrei Ustinov, Russian-American Company employes Fedor Kolmakov, Petr Gorokhov, and Gavril Patykov, together with twenty-nine Aleuts (Berkh, 1823, p. 46). The major aims of the expedition were to establish a redoubt at the mouth of the Nushagak River and, oddly enough, to investigate rumors that white men were living on the "Khiuveran" River, presumably somewhere on Seward Peninsula (Tikhmenev, 1939-40, p. 1, p. 300; DRHA,[1] vol. 3, p. 258; Berkh, 1823, fn., p. 49; Chernenko, 1956, fn. 4, pp. 16-17). At least one contemporary historian believed that these white men, if they were discovered, would turn out to be descendants of members of the Deshnev expedition which passed through Bering Strait in 1648 (Berkh, 1823).

Most of the Korsakovski expedition proceeded from Kodiak to Cook Inlet and traveled overland to Iliamna Lake in the spring of 1818. From there the route led down the Kvichak River to Bristol Bay and along the coast to the mouth of the Nushagak River. It seems probable that they explored the mouth of the river and not

[1] This is a reference to "Documents Relative to the History of Alaska," fifteen typewritten volumes, copies of which are located in the University of Alaska Library and the Library of Congress. These volumes, the first four of which contain most of the Russian era materials, were compiled as part of the Alaska History Research Project (1936-1938) of the University of Alaska.

merely the bay since in Ustinov's journal, which was never published but apparently accessible to Berkh, he refers to the large number of salmon to be seen at the mouth of the Aleknagik (Wood) River (Berkh, 1823, p. 48). Some of the party were left at the mouth of the Nushagak to construct a fortification, while Korsakovski and the others proceeded in baidarkas to the mouth of the Togiak River and Hagemeister Strait. Here Ustinov, in the cutter *Constantine*, waited for them with supplies that would be used for the exploration of the Kuskokwim River. After rounding Cape Newenham, the expedition approached the broad estuary of the Kuskokwim River but appears to have proceeded no farther than Goodnews Bay (Berkh, 1823, p. 46). Goodnews Bay and Cape Constantine, the western point of entrance to Nushagak Bay, and probably Hagemeister Strait were named by the Korsakovski expedition (Berkh, 1823, p. 46; Baker, 1902, p. 136).

The summer seems to have been well advanced by the time Korsakovski and Ustinov reached Goodnews Bay, and the Eskimos they met there advised them not to attempt to ascend the Kuskokwim River as they would encounter many hardships and would have difficulty in obtaining food (Tikhmenev, 1939-40, pt. 1, pp. 301-302). Some of the party, perhaps the Aleut interpreters and hunters, were probably unwilling to continue (DRHA, vol. 3, p. 358). In any case, the expedition turned back. Fedor Kolmakov had been left in charge of the party building the redoubt at the mouth of the Nushagak River, and the work had been completed by the time Korsakovski returned. The site selected was a high bluff along the east bank of Nushagak Bay about eight miles below the actual mouth of the river. The redoubt was named Alexandrovski, perhaps in honor of the Tsar, and Kolmakov already had established trade relations with the Eskimos living in the neighborhood (Tikhmenev, 1939-40, pt. 1, pp. 301-302). Unfortunately, no accurate description of the earliest construction at Nushagak is known to exist. It is not even certain whether Kolmakov remained at the post when other members of the expedition crossed the Alaska Peninsula and returned to Kodiak in the fall of 1818 (Chernenko, 1956, footnote 1, p. 16). It seems probable that he did, however, and possibly other members of the expedition remained with him. A census taken in January, 1819, indicates that three Russian men and two women were at Alexandrovski, but no population figures are given for Eskimos resident in the surrounding area (Tikhemenev, 1939-40, pt. 1, p. 306).

Whether or not he was actually a member of the Korsakovski expedition, Yanovski, Hagemeister's assistant at Sitka, seems to have taken considerable interest in its results. In two reports to the Board of Directors of the Russian-American Company, submitted in the spring of 1820, Yanovski recommended that the newly established Alexandrovski Redoubt be transferred to the mouth of the Kuskokwim River. This recommendation was apparently made because of the physical drawbacks of the new location, particularly the shallowness and treacherous shoals of the river immediately in front of the redoubt. In a letter dated March 15, 1821, from the Board of Directors to Matvei Ivanovich Muraviev, General Manager of the Russian-American Company, a clear decision was reached not to move the Nushagak station. The directors pointed out that since Alexandrovski had already been supplied by ship, it would be unnecessary to send a ship there each year. The redoubt could be supplied from Cook Inlet, and furs from the region could be transhipped in the opposite direction via Iliamna Lake. They further noted that it would probably be easier for the Kuskokwim Eskimos to trade at the mouth of the Nushagak River; in addition, fish and game of all kinds were plentiful there. Other justifications for not making the move included the unknown conditions of the Kuskokwim, and the rumor that the lower reaches of that river were treeless, rendering it difficult to construct a trading station. In addition it was thought that the mouth of the Kuskokwim could be reached only by way of the sea, and the large number of Eskimos resident in that area were not known to be peaceful and amenable to having a trading station near their villages. Thus the directors finally decided to postpone the transfer of their one Bering Sea trading station until the Kuskokwim River could be more thoroughly explored. Some interest was shown, however, in establishing a settlement on Hagemeister Island because of the rumored existence of large numbers of sea otters and fur seals in the area (DRHA, vol. 2, pp. 243-244).

In 1821-1822 the Russians made other attempts to learn more about the Bristol Bay region and to penetrate the Kuskokwim River system. In the first year the Russian-American Company outfitted an expedition under the direction of naval officers Adolf Karlovich Etolin and Vasili Stepanovich Khromchenko to survey the west Alaskan coast and the islands between Cape Newenham and Norton Sound and to gain knowledge of the inhabitants of the area. Information on this first expedition is extremely thin, at least as far as the Nushagak River region is concerned. Two ships were involved, the cutter *Baranov* under the command of Etolin, and the brig *Golovin,* commanded by Khromchenko. Their joint work consisted in making a survey of Hagemeister Strait and Island. Etolin, apparently before his first meeting with Khromchenko at Hagemeister Strait, surveyed the mouth of the Nushagak River and then later explored the lower part of the Kuskokwim (Tikhmenev, 1939-40, pt. 1, pp. 331-332; Russian-American Company Records: Communications Received, vol. 6, no. 346, folio 102).

The second expedition, during the summer of 1822, continued the 1821 survey, but this time only the *Golovin* was used and both officers were aboard; Khromchenko seems to have been in command (Burykin, 1957, p. 80). The party proceeded from Sitka to the Nushagak River, arriving at Alexandrovski Redoubt about the fourteenth of May. Here Khromchenko expected to find Fedor Kolmakov but he was told that the latter was trading with Eskimos at the mouth of the Togiak River. They eventually met at that point while the expedition was conducting surveys off Hagemeister Island (Khromchenko, 1824, pt. 10, pp. 275, 306). On the twenty-eighth of May, Khromchenko entered Nushagak Bay for the second time and anchored off the village of Ekuk. Up to that time he had apparently considered the possibility of a trip up the river in the brig but because of the extent of silt deposits and the shallowness of the bay in the vicinity of Ekuk, he decided that this voyage would be "inconvenient." In fact, he did not even attempt to proceed to Alexandrovski Redoubt in the *Golovin,* but transported his crew and equipment by small boat. Having unloaded his supplies, Khromchenko wished to leave Nushagak Bay at once, but was prevented from doing so by fog and bad weather. He finally departed on the ninth of June. In his journal Khromchenko mentioned that, according to information he obtained at the redoubt, the banks of the Nushagak River were heavily populated. He predicted a brilliant future for the fur trade in this area in spite of some unspecified trouble with the river Eskimos (Khromchenko, 1824, pt. 10, pp. 308, 314; pt. 11, pp. 38-40, 49).

At the time of the construction of Alexandrovski Redoubt in 1818, Fedor Kolmakov, of mixed Russian and aboriginal American ancestry, was put in charge of the new station. Because he established trade relations with the neighboring Eskimos and even baptized some of them, he was extremely useful in spreading the Russian-American Company's influence in the general area of the post. However, information about the people of the interior was very difficult to obtain. Kolmakov questioned Eskimos who came to the trading post from that area but since much of the trading with interior people was done through middlemen, most of the reports about the country and its inhabitants were conflicting (Tikhmenev, 1939-40, pt. 1, pp. 339-340).

Consequently, when Lieutenant Petr Egorovich Chistyakov succeeded Muraviev as the senior administrative officer of the Russian-American Company, it was decided to send an overland expedition under the leadership of Ivan Filippovich Vasiliev to explore the country north of Alexandrovski Redoubt, to make geographical and ethnological observations, and to establish trade relations with the Eskimos. Vasiliev set out from the redoubt in June of 1829 and ascended the Nushagak River. He was accompanied by three Russians, six Aleuts from Kodiak Island, and ten "baptized Aglegmiuts" whose loyalty was assured by the simple expediency of taking their families and keeping them as hostages at the redoubt (Zagoskin, 1956, p. 293). Vasiliev's route beyond the lower river is partly conjectural, but he appears to have followed a western tributary of the Nushagak, possibly the Nuyakuk, and to have explored Tikchik Lake and Lake Chauekuktuli. The Aglegmiuts who had accompanied him to act as guides became fearful as they neared the territory of the Kuskowagamiut and eventually refused to proceed further. Vasiliev stopped at a Kuskowagamiut settlement called Tuksa (probably the now abandoned village of Tikchik near the mouth of the Tikchik River) and attempted to persuade some of the inhabitants to guide him across the mountains to the Kuskokwim River. This they refused to do and the party was forced to return to Alexandrovski (Tikhmenev, 1939-40, pt. 1, pp. 339-341; Russian-American Company

Records: Communications Sent, vol. 6, no. 244, folio 478). The Russian priest Ivan Veniaminov, while visiting the redoubt in the summer of 1829, learned of this undertaking but was not in the area long enough to obtain information on the final outcome of the expedition. He was told, however, that Vasiliev had reached the "source" of the Nushagak which, at that time, was apparently believed to be Tikchik Lake (Barsukov, 1897-1901, vol. 1, p. 15).[2] Tebenkov's map of the area, dated 1849, suggests that the Nuyakuk and upper Nushagak were, indeed, confused. Although the cartouche obscures much of the river on the map, it is nevertheless shown flowing out of a lake to the west, undoubtedly Tikchik Lake but labeled Nushagak Lake (Tebenkov, 1852, chart 4—Bristol Bay). During the late summer of 1829, Vasiliev made further explorations to the west and northwest of Alexandrovski Redoubt, ascending the Wood River and exploring one or more of the Wood River Lakes (Tikhmenev, 1939-40, pt. 1, p. 341; Russian-American Company Records: Communications Sent, vol. 6, no. 244, folio 482).

The following summer, in 1830, Vasiliev again attempted to reach the Kuskokwim River by way of the Nushagak. This time he was successful. Leaving Alexandrovski Redoubt on June 19, his party ascended the river to its headwaters, crossed over to the Holitna in an "agonizing five day march," and descended that stream to the Kuskokwim. Although Vasiliev's orders included an instruction to explore the Yukon River, he found it impossible to obtain guides and supplies and decided not to proceed. The return trip was made down the Kuskokwim and around the coast to Alexandrovski (Russian-American Company Records: Communications Sent, vol. 7, no. 257, folio 269).

Two years later, in 1832, Fedor Kolmakov and Semen Lukin, a mixed-blood employe at the redoubt and an interpreter for the Vasiliev party, made a similar trip with a party of six Eskimos.

[2] Veniaminov's letter to the Russian geographer and explorer, Fedor Petrovich Litke, from which this information is taken, is dated June 3, 1828. This is presumed to be an error. All other sources for the Vasiliev explorations mention them as having taken place in 1829 and 1830. Veniaminov himself mentions elsewhere (Barsukov, 1886-88, vol 2, p. 37) that he visited Alexandrovski Redoubt for the first time in the summer of 1829.

They founded the first trading station on the Kuskokwim, a single cabin built at the confluence of the Holitna and the Kuskokwim (Zagoskin, 1956, pp. 46, 258; Russian-American Company Records: Communications Sent, vol. 9, no. 321, folios 482-487; no. 555, folio 444). This post was abandoned after a year because it proved to be located too far inland to be convenient for trading with the central Kuskokwim River people. In 1833 Kolmakov supervised the construction of a second post, this time at the small Eskimo and Ingalik Indian village of Kvigimpainagmiut, on the northeast bank of the Kuskokwim, at the mouth of the Kwik River (Tikhmenev, 1939-40, pt. 1, p. 341; VanStone, 1959, p. 46, footnote 28). Lukin used these posts seasonally in his trading activities.

The third and last trading station in this central Kuskokwim River region was built across the river from Kvigimpainagmiut in 1841 and consisted of a group of rather elaborate log structures. Fedor Kolmakov had died in 1839 so the new post was given the status of a redoubt and named in his honor (Zagoskin, 1956, p. 259; Russian-American Company Records: Communications Sent, vol. 17, no. 509, folio 493). It remained an important trading center until abandoned by the Russian-American Company in 1866.

The exploration of Bristol Bay and the lower Nushagak River, together with the founding of Alexandrovski Redoubt, later called Nushagak by Anglo-Americans, played a vital role in opening up the interior regions of southwestern Alaska to the fur trade. Kolmakovski Redoubt continued to be supplied from Alexandrovski, at least until 1845, and the route from the headwaters of the Nushagak River, across the divide and down the Holitna or Hoholitna to the Kuskokwim became a heavily traveled route with supplies going upriver into the Kuskokwim country and furs proceeding in the opposite direction. The entire early history of Russian activity on the Kuskokwim is closely tied to Alexandrovski Redoubt (see Oswalt, 1963, ch. 1; Chernenko, 1956).

After 1841, Russian Orthodox missionaries also penetrated the Nushagak River country. Unfortunately, little is known of either the trading or the missionary explorations; and the exact nature of the earliest contacts between the Russians and Nushagak Eskimos remains largely a matter of conjecture. Mikhailovski Redoubt, established north of the mouth of the Yukon in 1833, reduced to a large extent the importance of Alexandrovski. More about this will be said in connection with the history of trading activities in the Nushagak River region. It is sufficient to note here that Alexandrovski's importance for inland trading activity appears to have lasted for less than twenty-five years. However, at the time of the Western Union Telegraph Expedition in 1865, the mail was carried overland from St. Michael every winter to Nushagak and then sent by ship to Sitka. Even Kolmakovski Redoubt seems to have maintained some contact with Nushagak, as Dall mentions that winter mail to and from the former post was carried overland following the route pioneered by Vasiliev and Lukin (Dall, 1870, pp. 273-274).

A rough idea of the extent to which the Nushagak River region had become known geographically as a result of the earliest Russian penetration can be gained from three contemporary maps, the first published in 1841, the second in 1847-48, and the third dated 1849. The earliest map, already referred to, accompanies Ternaux-Compans' summary of the explorations of Andrei Glazunov. This map shows the Nushagak River and its major western tributary, the Nuyakuk, with the latter flowing, as it does, out of Tikchik Lake which is located well to the west in an approximately correct position (VanStone, 1959, p. 38). However, one receives a definite impression from this map that the Nushagak and Nuyakuk are believed to be one river. The Nushagak north of the mouth of the Nuyakuk is given a new name, the "Ilgajak" and appears to have been considered a Nushagak tributary. This river rises in the Nushagak Hills and is the "Ilgayak" River referred to by Zagoskin (1956, map) on which was located a Russian trail house used to facilitate the movement of supplies and furs overland to the Kuskokwim (Zagoskin, 1956, pp. 261-262). The Ternaux-Compans map accurately indicates the extent of Nushagak Bay and shows the Wood River flowing out of Lake Aleknagik.

On the Zagoskin map of 1847-48 Nushagak Bay, the Wood River, and Lake Aleknagik are also shown accurately, as is Tikchik Lake, but the latter is referred to as Nushagak Lake.

The 1849 map is a chart of Bristol Bay in Tebenkov's (1852) atlas of the northwest coast of America. Nushagak Bay and river are shown on this map as is the Wood River and Wood River Lakes. As previously mentioned, the cartouche obscures much of the river on this map, but it is obvious that, again, the Nuyakuk and upper Nushagak are confused, and Tikchik Lake is called Nushagak Lake.

✱ The maps show that the explorations of Vasiliev, Kolmakov, and Lukin did a great deal to acquaint the Russians with the geography of the Nushagak River region, at least in broad outline, and subsequent journeys of missionaries and other traders undoubtedly extended knowledge. Nevertheless, it is true that except for the broad outlines, the Nushagak area was almost unknown to the Russians at the time of the sale of Alaska to the United States in 1867, and it was to remain unknown to its new American owners until almost the turn of the century✱

For long after the transfer of Alaska from Russia to the United States, no attempt was made to explore the Nushagak River region. Traders and Russian Orthodox missionaries still made their way up the river and to various points in the bay area, but the United States government confined its activities to occasional visits of vessels to Nushagak. Captain J. W. White, in command of the United States Revenue Steamer *Wayanda*, must have been one of the first government employes to visit Nushagak after the purchase. He arrived in June, 1868, but did not attempt to ascend the river. He simply visited the redoubt (or fort as it is usually called in sources of the American period), noted that the assets of the Russian-American Company had been transferred to Hutchison, Kohl and Company of San Francisco, and mentioned the decaying buildings of the Russian redoubt (White, 1869, p. 6).

In 1886 the Moravian Church established a mission station at the mouth of the Nushagak River, just north of Nushagak. This mission was called Carmel and within a few years Moravian influence spread up the Nushagak River for a distance of at least eighty miles, and the missionaries also traveled along the coast westward in the direction of the Togiak River and Goodnews Bay (Schwalbe, 1951, pp. 51-52).

Nushagak was one of the early stations of the Signal Service of the United States Army in Alaska. This program was initiated largely through the efforts of Spencer Baird, at that time Secretary of the Smithsonian Institution. The observers selected for these stations were young men interested in all aspects of natural history and qualified to make good use of the time they would have when not carrying out their meteorological duties. One of these observers was Edward William Nelson and during his tour of duty at St. Michael he made the fine collection of ethnological specimens from western Alaska, a collection so large and important that it has made Nelson's name familiar to all subsequent students of Alaskan ethnology and archaeology. Under orders issued in the spring of 1881, Charles L. McKay was sent to establish the station at Nushagak. For two years he spent much of his time on natural history work but in the spring of 1883, he was drowned in the bay under mysterious circumstances. McKay was succeeded by J. W. Johnson who remained until 1886 (Osgood, 1904, pp. 25-26).

McKay apparently made a number of trips from Nushagak although no first-hand information exists concerning his activities. He is said to have ascended the Wood River to Lake Alegnagik and he also apparently visited Iliamna Lake and Lake Clark. At least this information was related to Wilfred H. Osgood in 1902 by an Eskimo at Nushagak (Osgood, 1904, pp. 25-26). The visit to Lake Clark at this early date is of particular interest. The presence of a large lake in the general region had been known for a long time (Townsend and Townsend, 1961, p. 55, footnote 2) and is present, though unnamed, on the Ternaux-Compans, Tebenkov, and Zagoskin maps (VanStone, 1959, p. 38; Tebenkov, 1852, Chart 4; Zagoskin, 1956). McKay is sometimes described as the European discoverer of Lake Clark, although it is almost certain that some Russian party visited the lake during the late eighteenth or early nineteenth century.

The year 1890 marks the beginning of more extensive and intensive exploration of the Nushagak River region, both along the coast and into the interior. However, even before that year, in 1887-88, a party of prospectors who had been working on the upper Yukon came down that river, crossed to the Kuskokwim, traveled along part of the Bering Sea and Bristol Bay coast, and ascended the Nushagak and the Mulchatna rivers as far as the mouth of the Kakhtul River. Here the party, which consisted of Percy Walker, Henry Melish, and Al King, placer mined for gold on a cut bank near the mouth of the river, but the gold they found was too fine and flaky to save (Anonymous, 1921, p. 1; Spurr, 1900, pp. 95-96).

After having worked south of the Alaska Peninsula during the summers of 1888 and 1889, the United States Fish Commission Steamer *Albatross,* during the summers of 1890 and 1891, completed a preliminary survey in the southwestern part of Bering Sea from Unalaska to the head of Bristol Bay and Cape Newenham. The work consisted mostly of reconnaissance of the shoreline. Soundings were taken, records of currents, wind, and weather were kept, and a considerable amount of geographical information was obtained. This was the first detailed survey of the Bristol Bay region and the information gathered was used in subsequent editions of the *Alaska Coast Pilot* (Tanner, 1891, p. 279).

During the summer of 1890, while the *Albatross* was anchored in Nushagak Bay, Ivan Petroff, the enumerator of the Tenth Federal Census in 1880, came on board with three Eskimo assistants. Petroff, who had visited Nushagak ten years earlier while collecting data for the first United States census to include Alaska, had now just returned from an unsuccessful attempt to reach the Kuskokwim River by way of the inland route up the Nushagak River and over the portage to the Holitna, the route pioneered by Vasiliev and Lukin. Petroff apparently made the attempt in connection with his census duties for the Eleventh Census. However, he chose the wrong time of the year—late May shortly after breakup—and as a result he had to work his way laboriously up the river against a strong current. He proceeded well beyond the mouth of the Mulchatna and seems to have been approaching the portage when his party refused to proceed and he was forced to return. Once on board the *Albatross,* he requested transportation to Cape Newenham from which point he expected to be able to reach the Eskimo villages on the Kuskokwim River (Tanner, 1893, p. 229; Petroff, 1891, p. 2).

A more successful trip, which actually contributed to the geographical knowledge of the Nushagak River region, was made in the winter of 1891 by a party under the leadership of Alfred B. Schanz and sponsored by *Frank Leslie's Illustrated Newspaper.* This expedition, which consisted of Schanz, John W. Clark, agent of the Alaska Commercial Company at Nushagak, and seven Eskimos, left Nushagak on January 29 and ascended the Nushagak River, taking the census of the villages along the route. They then proceeded up the Mulchatna River to the Kakhtul River, ascended that tributary and, making a portage, reached the Chulitna

River which flowed into a large lake that they named Lake Clark. Quite conceivably, with the possible exception of Charles L. McKay, the members of the Schanz expedition were the first non-Russian white men to see this important lake. The expedition returned by way of Iliamna Lake, the Kvichak River, and around the coast to Nushagak (Porter, 1893, p. 94; Schanz, 1891, pp. 138-139; Mertie, 1938, pp. 4-5).

In the same year William C. Greenfield, also compiling information for the Eleventh Census, ascended the Holitna River from the Kuskokwim, portaged to the Chichitnok, a headwater tributary of the Nushagak, and descended the main river to Nushagak (Mertie, 1938, pp. 4-5). Since Greenfield was not responsible for collecting census data on the Nushagak, little published information records that part of his trip. It is claimed that his journey, which followed the same route as that taken by Lukin in 1832, was the first made over the route by a white man since Vasiliev (Spurr, 1900, p. 100). However, many Russians made the trip during the period when furs were being shipped from Kolmakovski Redoubt by way of Alexandrovski Redoubt.

It should be kept in mind that the Russian priests and, from 1886, Moravian missionaries, continued to make trips up the Nushagak River and its main tributaries throughout the latter part of the nineteenth century and, of course, into the twentieth. These trips, however, added little to the general knowledge of the Nushagak River region; and the written reports of the missionaries, both published and archival, while valuable from the standpoint of church history, usually say little or nothing about the geographical features or problems of travel, and often little enough about settlement patterns and the Eskimo communities. After the Russian Orthodox and Moravian churches entered into competition in the region, the number of trips into the surrounding area probably were increased as each church sought to extend its own influence or neutralize the influence of the other. Thus, in 1895-96, John H. Schoechert, a Moravian missionary from Carmel, mentions that his Orthodox counterpart would often follow him up the Nushagak River, visit the same villages, rebaptize the children, and sell holy pictures. During that year Schoechert made eight trips up the river and to Togiak. Seven of these trips involved traveling from 200 to 400 miles by dog team or in a baidarka, while the longest trip was more than 800 miles and took twenty-three days (SPG Proceedings, 1896, pp. 27-28).[3]

During a reconnaissance in southwestern Alaska in 1898, the geologist Josiah E. Spurr visited the upper part of Nushagak Bay but did not ascend the river. His party followed a well-traveled route from Kulukak Bay to Nushagak Bay, a valuable route because it avoids the long and sometimes dangerous journey around Cape Constantine (Spurr, 1900, pp. 89, 99).

By the end of the nineteenth century, the general character of the coastal sections of the Nushagak region was reasonably well known. Not only was there the work of the *Albatross*, but in the meantime Bristol Bay had become an important salmon fishing location; and as the fishing industry grew, so did settlements of white people and Eskimos in the bay area. The vast inland region north of Bristol Bay, however, remained comparatively unknown although it continued to be visited by occasional traders and trappers, missionaries, and prospectors. The activities of the latter in particular seemed to increase even though the Nushagak River region never became an important gold mining area. Nevertheless, gold miners played an important role in opening up the Mulchatna and upper Nushagak River country.

A survey for a railroad line from Iliamna Bay to Anvik on the Yukon was begun in 1901 and continued, more or less actively, for several years. A route eventually was selected but no construction was ever undertaken. Apparently the route was to run westward up the valley of the Chulitna River and the crude exploratory survey may have reached the upper Mulchatna but did not involve the area of this study (Smith, 1917, p. 15; Capps, 1931, pp. 126-127). However, in December of the same year a party traveled overland from Iliamna Lake, down the Mulchatna and Nushagak rivers, conducting a survey to determine the feasibility of inaugurating a winter sled line, to be operated with horses, and to have roadhouses at intervals. The survey was apparently sponsored by a "Trans-Alaska Company" but nothing ever came of the venture (Shawhan, 1902, p. 511).

Much more significant inland explorations were made by

[3] This is a reference to the annual *Proceedings of the Society of the United Brethren for Propagating the Gospel among the Heathen,* published by the Moravian Church at Bethlehem, Pennsylvania.

Wilfred H. Osgood during the summer of 1902 for the United States Department of Agriculture, Division of Biological Survey. Osgood and a small party, landing at Iliamna Bay, crossed the mountains to Iliamna Lake, and proceeded to Lake Clark. The group journeyed up the Chulitna River and from there crossed to Swan Lake and descended the Swan River and the Kakhtul and Nushagak rivers. Osgood's report contains valuable material on settlement patterns and movements of people in the area (Osgood, 1904).

Beginning in the summer of 1907, members of the United States Bureau of Fisheries visited the Wood River Lakes, the Nushagak and Nuyakuk rivers, and the lower Tikchik Lakes in connection with studies related to salmon spawning. In that year a preliminary exploration was made of the Wood River and Lake Aleknagik for the purpose of making counts of salmon escaping up the Wood River. During the summers of 1908 and 1909, an agent of the Bureau of Fisheries examined every stream tributary to the lake. This was the beginning of an intensive exploration of the entire lakes region during which every inch of the shorelines of these lakes seems to have been examined. Unfortunately, no comparable amount of exploration seems to have been carried out on the Nushagak River. The Bureau of Fisheries reports, despite the occasional reference to an Eskimo village or archaeological site, contain, with one important exception, practically no information about the inhabitants of the area or any aspect of the subsistence fishery (Mertie, 1938, pp. 4-5; Marsh and Cobb, 1911b, p. 37).

The exception referred to documents the work of Ward T. Bower during the late summer of 1923 when he examined the spawning grounds in the Tikchik Lakes. To reach these lakes a trip was made by boat up the Nushagak and Nuyakuk rivers. Bower's report is particularly valuable for the information it provides concerning the occupied villages on the Nushagak River at that time. His detailed map, showing the locations of these villages, is also extremely useful (Bower, 1926, pp. 108-110).

In June, 1931 the anthropologist Aleš Hrdlička ascended the Nushagak River as far as Old Koliganek and then traveled up the Mulchatna to a point not far beyond the mouth of the Kakhtul River (Hrdlička, 1944). The primary purpose of his trip was to collect skeletal material for the United States National Museum, and he also located and described a large number of archaeo-logical sites. His work is significant since he was the first anthro-pologist to work in the area, but his statements about sites and their locations are extremely vague. (Many could not be located or accurately identified during the author's survey in the summer of 1964.) Hrdlička has little to say about inhabited settlements, although his description of one village on the lower Mulchatna is very valuable.

The final explorations to be discussed here were carried out in 1935 for the United States Geological Survey by John B. Mertie. At that time the relative isolation of the Bristol Bay region was beginning to break down and a weekly air service operated be-tween Anchorage and the bay community of Dillingham. The Mertie party thoroughly explored the entire region considered in this study together with the Wood River Lakes, the Tikchik Lakes, the Nushagak Hills, and the upper Mulchatna River. Mer-tie's report deals mainly with the geology of the region, but it also contains important historical data as well as much information on the native inhabitants and settlements in the area. It is without doubt the standard reference on the Nushagak River region (Mer-tie, 1938).

The modern trends noted by Mertie and just beginning at the time of his explorations in the early 1930's have, of course, con-tinued. The community of Nushagak, site of the old Alexan-drovski Redoubt, began to decline shortly after the turn of the century and is now abandoned. Rival villages grew up on the west shore of Nushagak Bay; and one of these, Dillingham, after a varied past, has emerged as the cosmopolitan trading center for the Bristol Bay and Nushagak River region. Instead of the newly inaugurated weekly flights of Mertie's time, Anchorage and Dill-ingham are now connected by a fast, daily prop-jet service. In common with many other areas of Alaska, the bush air services that began in the late 1920's and early 1930's opened up the inte-rior north of Nushagak Bay and have proliferated since the Sec-ond World War to the point where, in winter, the Nushagak River communities enjoy daily mail and freight service with ser-vice three times a week in summer. The commercial fishing indus-try, a major economic factor in the Nushagak River region since the 1880's, is still, in spite of many ups and downs, important to the people of the area and the frantic seasonal activity gives the bay area the characteristic way of life that it has known for nearly eighty years.

It is now time to examine in detail the activities of those who followed and, in some cases, accompanied the explorers. They were, for the most part, more interested in the local inhabitants, their customs, and the possibility of trading with them, converting them, or improving their way of life, than in the country itself. The explorers were the spearhead of contact and their efforts were always intimately related to the activities of those to whom we now turn, the agents of culture change.

II

Missionary Activity

◇◆

◦NO INNOVATION AMONG THE ESKIMOS OF THE NUSHAGAK RIVER RE-
gion has had a greater or more lasting effect than Christianity.◦
Furthermore, the Russian Orthodox Church, the pioneer denomination in the area, played a role at least equal to that of the Russian-American Company in opening up the country and in exposing the people to outside influences. Later, for a short period at
the end of the nineteenth century and the beginning of the twentieth, the Moravian Church enacted a similar role. Our purpose
here is to discuss the spread of Christianity in the Nushagak River
region focusing on relations between the missionaries and their
Eskimo converts.

Christianity was introduced to the Nushagak River region at
the time of the construction of Alexandrovski Redoubt in 1818
and during the next ten years there is evidence that Fedor Kolmakov, the creole trader in charge of the post, baptized a small
number of Eskimos who were employes in the service of the Russian-American Company at the redoubt (Barsukov, 1887-1888,
vol. 2, p. 36). No priest, however, had visited Kolmakov's small
settlement nor did one come until 1829.

After 1821, the year the Russian-American Company received
its second charter from the Tsar, several priests were sent from
Irkutsk in Siberia to Alaska at the request of the Company's administration. Among those was a young priest, Father Ivan Veniaminov, who sailed first to Sitka and then to Unalaska in 1823. At
that time, or shortly thereafter, the missionary activities in Rus-

sian America were divided among four priests whose headquarters were at Sitka, on Kodiak Island, and on Unalaska and Atka.
The church on Unalaska, replacing an earlier chapel, had been
constructed in 1825-1826, and its territory included the Fox and
Pribilof islands as well as Alexandrovski, and later, Mikhailovski
redoubts (Tikhmenev, 1939-1940, pt. 2, pp. 350-351) (see map 1).
From the time of his first arrival in Alaska, Veniaminov had a
great desire to spread Christianity in the vast area north of the
Alaska Peninsula, to see what the country was like, and to learn
about the people who lived there. Consequently he asked and received permission from the Bishop of Irkutsk to make a trip to
the region (Barsukov, 1887-1888, vol. 2, p. 36).

In the spring of 1829 Father Veniaminov arrived at Alexandrovski Redoubt to visit the few Christians, Russians, and mixed-
bloods living there. At that time there were fourteen Eskimos at
the redoubt who had come to trade. Veniaminov immediately set
about attempting to convert them since it seemed unlikely that he
would be able to travel in the area and meet more people. He
succeeded in baptizing thirteen of the visitors and noted that "the
Nushagak River was for them the river Jordan" (Barsukov,
1887-1888, vol. 2, p. 37). The priest presented each baptized Eskimo with a copper cross but did not give them any other gifts. He
feared that if he distributed gifts freely, the Eskimos would present themselves to the next clergyman who visited the area in
order to receive more. When he departed from the redoubt, Veniaminov authorized Kolmakov to baptize those Eskimos who
might come to the post to inquire about Christianity, but he
warned that under no circumstances were gifts to be given to the
new converts (Barsukov, 1887-1888, vol. 2, p. 37).

In 1832 Veniaminov again visited the redoubt, this time in the
company of Ferdinand Petrouich Wrangell, general manager of
the Russian-American Company who was making a tour of inspection. The priest learned that since his first visit Fedor Kolmakov had baptized 70 Eskimos from various villages at the request of the converts. Some of these were present at the redoubt
and Veniaminov preached to them and administered the Holy
Sacraments in the presence of the general manager. Wrangell was
apparently impressed, for he ordered the construction of a small
chapel which was completed in 1832 (Barsukov, 1887-1888, vol. 2,

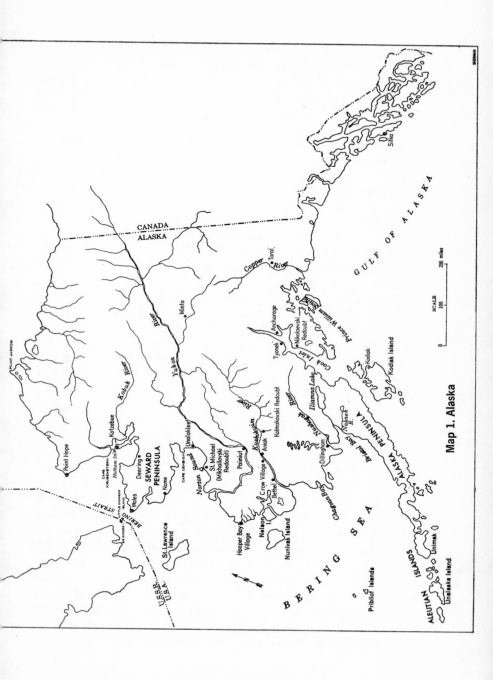

Map 1. Alaska

pp. 37-38; Russian-American Company Records: Communications Sent, vol. 9, no. 460, folio 350; vol. 14, no. 244, folios 274-275; vol. 19, no. 147, folio 186). Veniaminov was pleased with the increase in church membership since his previous visit. Furthermore some of the men he had baptized in 1829 heard of his arrival and brought their families to be baptized.

Between 1832 and 1838, Fedor Kolmakov and his son Petr baptized at least 62 individuals and probably more. However, they seem to have done this reluctantly, either on the grounds that they were not clergymen, or because they were not impressed with the ability of the Eskimos to practice a Christian way of life. In 1838 Gregory Golovin, Veniaminov's successor as the clergyman of the Unalaska church, visited the redoubt and administered the Sacraments to 53 of those baptized by the Kolmakovs and, in addition, baptized 52 new converts (Barsukov, 1887-1888, vol. 2, p. 38).

After his two visits to Alexandrovski Redoubt, Veniaminov was very optimistic that Christianity would spread among the Eskimos north of the Alaska Peninsula. On the basis of his observations at the redoubt, the priest concluded that the Eskimos of the region would receive baptism willingly and that any priest who visited the people would not have to convince them of the value and worth of Christianity, but merely teach them and, through the administering of the Sacraments, strengthen them in their resolve to lead Christian lives. Veniaminov further concluded that the people of the Nushagak region were peaceable and kindhearted and that missionaries would meet little or no opposition provided the churchmen "act in the spirit of the Apostles" (Barsukov, 1887-1888, vol. 2, pp. 39-40; 1897-1901, vol. 1, p. 14).

By 1834 Father Veniaminov had been transferred from Unalaska to Sitka. In 1840 the Holy Synod decided to create out of Russia's possessions in the North Pacific a see to be known as the Diocese of Kamchatka, the Aleutian, and Kurile Islands. Veniaminov was named bishop, and in accordance with ecclesiastical practice he took monastic vows and underwent tonsure. He also adopted the name of Innokentii. Because of his interest in the Nushagak River region, one of Veniaminov's first acts as bishop was to request permission from the Holy Synod to establish a mission at Alexandrovski Redoubt. A ukase of January 10, 1841, authorized him to establish the first Russian Orthodox Church north of the Alaska Peninsula. In November of the same year Deacon Ilia Petelin, Veniaminov's son-in-law, who years before had come with the new bishop from Irkutsk, was ordained a priest and appointed to take charge of the Nushagak mission. The new missionary, his song leader, Vasili Shishkin, and their families, left Sitka for Kodiak in February, 1842, departed from that settlement in June of the same year, and arrived at Nushagak on July 19 (DRHA, vol. 1, pp. 385-386; Russian-American Company Records: Communications Sent, vol. 21, no. 28, folio 25; vol. 21, no. 30, folio 27).

It is also possible that A. K. Etolin, general manager of the Russian-American Company, had something to do with the establishment of a mission at Alexandrovski. On September 27, 1840, he wrote to the Company's main office in St. Petersburg that although many people in the vicinity of the redoubt had been baptized they had no real knowledge of Christian principles and could not be expected to have so long as they were visited only occasionally by a priest from Unalaska. Etolin's concern for the spiritual well-being of the Nushagak Eskimos was prompted by his belief that increased contact with Orthodox priests would make the people more friendly and trusting and thus easier to deal with for furs (Russian-American Company Records: Communications Sent, vol. 19, no. 147, folio 187).

The number of Christians at Nushagak in 1842 was about 200 and during the next three years as many as 400 additional Eskimos were baptized. According to the missionary's journal, which is quoted by Tikhmenev (1939-1940, pt. 2, pp. 297-298), the Eskimos gladly received Father Petelin and listened attentively to his preachings. To prove the sincerity of their conversion they even gathered up masks used in aboriginal ceremonies and burned them or threw them in the river. The priest was continually surprised by their piety, diligence, and understanding of the gospels. Father Petelin also seems to have widened the scope of his activities to include the regions north of the redoubt. He very probably went up the Nuskagak on several occasions and he visited the Kuskokwim in 1843 and received many Eskimos into the church (Zagoskin, 1956, footnote p. 46). This was doubtless the first visit by a priest to that river and from this time on any statistics given for church members associated with the Nushagak mission include residents of the Kuskokwim River as well.

In 1844 Bishop Veniaminov issued an order for the construction of a new church at Nushagak to replace the old chapel built in 1832. The following year, Father Petelin reported the church had been completed and dedicated to the Apostles Peter and Paul (DRHA, vol. 1, p. 387). Meanwhile, the Orthodox Church was increasing and extending its activities in southwestern Alaska. In the summer of 1843 Gregory Golovin of Unalaska visited the Mikhailovski Redoubt which had been founded in 1833. He suggested that a mission be founded there and Bishop Veniaminov sent Golovin to establish one in the spring of 1844 (DRHA, vol. 1, p. 362). In a report to the Holy Synod in April, 1842, the bishop also suggested organizing a new mission on Cook Inlet, but a missionary, Hieromonk Nikolai, did not reach Nikolaevski Redoubt until April, 1845 (DRHA, vol. 1, pp. 354-355).

In 1840 A. K. Etolin had become general manager of the Russian-American Company and he immediately moved to reduce the Company's expenditures by consolidating a number of the more remote posts. With this in mind he wrote to Bishop Veniaminov on December 23, 1844, explaining his plans which involved the entire southwestern Alaska region. The Alexandroviski Redoubt was to be eliminated and only an *odinochka* with one baidarka leader (*Baidarshchik*) and three or four "Aleuts" were to be left there. These men would be subordinated to Nikolaevski Redoubt from where they would be supplied with food and trade goods by way of a small post on Iliamna Lake. This plan would eliminate the use of sailing vessels in communicating with Nushagak. Furthermore, Kolmakovski Redoubt, which had been subordinated to Nushagak, would, in the future, be within the sphere of influence of Mikhailovski Redoubt (see maps 1 and 2). Etolin further requested Veniaminov to arrange matters in such a way that upon the establishment of a church at Nikolaevski Redoubt, which actually took place the following year, the priest would take charge of the church at Nushagak while the missionary at Mikhailovski Redoubt would take charge of all the converted Eskimos along the Kuskokwim River. This, according to Etolin, would relieve the Company of the delivery of large quantities of goods to Nushagak (DRHA, vol. 1, pp. 365-66; Russian-American

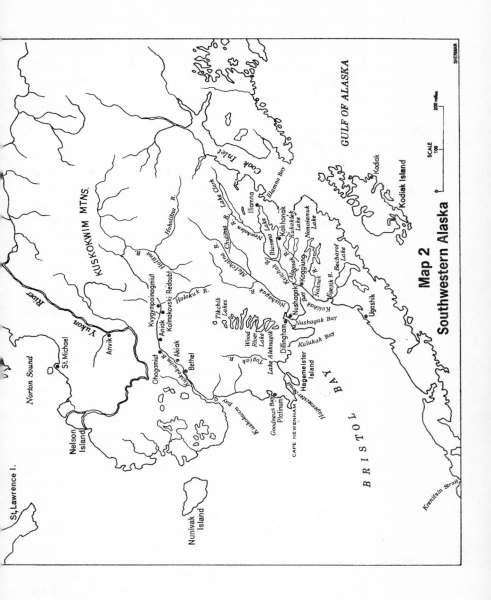

Map 2
Southwestern Alaska

St. Lawrence I.

Norton Sound

Nelson Island

Nunivak Island

Yukon River

St. Michael

Anvik

KUSKOKWIM MTNS.

Hoholitna R.

Holitna R.

Kvygympaingamiut

Aniak

Kolmakovski Redoubt

Holokuk R.

Ohogamiut

Kuskokwim R.

Akiak

Bethel

O Tikchik Lakes

Wood River Lake

Lake Aleknagik

Togiak R.

Kulukak Bay

Hagemeister Island

Hagemeister Strait

CAPE NEWENHAM

Goodnews Bay

Platinum

Kuskburne Bay

Lake Clark

Chulitna R.

Mulchatna R.

Newhalen R.

Nushagak R.

Koyokuk R.

Iliamna R.

Iliamna Lake

Iliamna

Iliamna Bay

Cook Inlet

Kakhonok

Kukaklek Lake

Nonvianuk Lake

Alagnak R.

Kvichak R.

Koggiung

Nushagak Bay

Dillingham

Nushagak Bay

Nushagak Bay

Naknek R.

Kvichak

Egegik R.

Becharof Lake

Ugashik

BRISTOL BAY

Krenitzin Strait

GULF OF ALASKA

Kodiak

Kodiak Island

SCALE
0   100   200 miles

SHERMAN

80306

Company Records: Communications Sent, vol. 23, no. 703, folio 554).

In a reply to Etolin's letter, written on January 9, 1845, Bishop Veniaminov consented to combining the Nushagak and Kenai missions. However, he warned that "because my instructions regarding the establishment of missions at Nushagak and Kenai are approved by the Holy Synod, I do not dare to issue orders for the discontinuance of Nushagak Mission until the circumstances show whether or not it will be possible for the Kenai missionary to visit Nushagak region at least once in two years." Wishing to coordinate his activities as much as possible with the interests of the Company in regard to the abolishment of the church at Nushagak, the bishop issued the following instructions: (1) he sent Hieromonk Nikolai and one churchman from Sitka to the Nikolaevski Redoubt as has previously been noted; (2) he ordered the Yukon missionary to take under his care all the people along the Kuskokwim and Holitna rivers, people who were formerly served by the Nushagak missionary; (3) he ordered the Nushagak missionary, presumably Father Petelin, to explore the route to Iliamna Lake; and (4) he ordered Nikolai to explore the route to the mouth of the Naknek River (DRHA, vol. 1, p. 372).

Father Petelin left the Nushagak mission for Kodiak in the summer of 1846 and Vasili Shishkin remained behind to take care of the church and celebrate divine services. Hieromonk Nikolai began his visits the following year (DRHA, vol. 1, p. 247; Barsukov, 1897-1901, vol. 1, p. 222; Russian-American Company Records: Communications Sent, vol. 26, no. 488, folios 381-382; vol. 27, no. 325, folio 463). In July, 1849, Veniaminov wrote to his superior, Philaret, Metropolitan of Moscow, that the Nushagak mission had been visited by "Kenai missionaries." The bishop also reported in the same letter that the mission was in a satisfactory condition and that the Eskimos attended services and had no inclination to perform ceremonies in secret.

Veniaminov was pleased to learn that a great many Eskimos came to the missionary from remote villages and that others sent messages requesting a visit from the priest. When the priest did make such trips, he was very well received. The Aglegmiuts are mentioned as being the most friendly of all and although their villages were some distance from the church, they were remarkably faithful in their church attendance on Sundays. However, Veniaminov felt called upon to mention that at one unidentified Kiatagmiut village not far from the mission, the missionary encountered considerable resistance. The villagers told him that they would not be baptized nor would they allow their children to be baptized. The village shaman in particular resented the exhortations of the missionary, but mostly older people were unreceptive to the teachings of the church. When the missionary had retired for the night, a number of young men visited him and offered their children for baptism. The bishop found this trend for young people to go against the wishes of their elders very encouraging. He must have been further encouraged by the fact that in 1848 there were 1,080 parishioners in the Nushagak region, a fact that suggests considerable activity by Orthodox missionaries on the Togiak and Kuskokwim rivers (Barsukov, 1897-1901, vol. 1, p. 222).

Hieromonk Nikolai resided at Nushagak from April, 1850, until the middle of May, 1851 (Barsukov, 1897-1901, vol. 1, p. 371). During this period he succeeded in visiting all the villages belonging to the mission and there is some indication that he was the first missionary to make an extensive trip up the Nushagak River. The church records for 1850 and 1851 suggest that at least one visit was made to the central river region and perhaps even to Tikchik Lake (Alaska Russian Church Archives, accession 12,766, vital statistics, Nushagak, 1850-1851). Again Veniaminov had cause to be optimistic in his letter to Philaret, written at Ayan in Siberia on June 25, 1852. At that time the Nushagak mission embraced 1,448 parishioners and the people continued to be friendly and receptive to Christian teaching. Even the residents of the recalcitrant Kiatagmiut settlement now rejected shamanism and accepted the missionary with "evident gladness" (Barsukov, 1897-1901, vol. 1, pp. 372-373).

When Nikolai departed in May, 1851, to return to his own church at Nikolaevski Redoubt, the Nushagak mission was once again in the charge of Vasili Shishkin. He was joined, in the summer of 1853, by Heiromonk Theophil; thus it seems that the church authorities, in spite of the suggestions made by Etolin for consolidating mission activity in southwestern Alaska, decided, after a brief interval, to maintain a priest at the Nushagak mission (Barsukov, 1897-1901, vol. 1, p. 407; Russian-American Company Records: Communications Sent, vol. 34, no. 382, folio 130).

For the decade between 1851 and 1861 information on activities at the Nushagak mission is scarce. It is known that in 1850 a house was built for the priest and another for his subordinate. This was presumably carried out under the direction of Nikolai (DRHA, vol. 1, p. 333). In 1860 a new church was built (DRHA, vol. 1, p. 387; Russian-American Company Records: Communications Sent, vol. 42, no. 53, folio 138) and one year later Nushagak is listed as being one of seven missionary districts in Alaska, the others being Sitka, Kodiak, Unalaska, Atka, Kenai, and the Yukon (Dall, 1870, p. 351).

Hieromonk Theophil, toward the end of his period of service at the Nushagak mission, reflected in his journal for 1862 and 1863 upon the success of his efforts to instill the principles of Christianity in the minds and hearts of the Eskimos whom he visited on his infrequent trips up the Nushagak River. His pessimistic comments contrast markedly with the cheerful optimism of Veniaminov thirty years earlier. Theophil complained that he could not see any good resulting from his trips to the four or five villages inhabited by Kiatagmiut, and he doubted whether much had been accomplished in the two- or three-day visits made by former missionaries or even in the five-day visits which he himself made. When he visited the villages, Theophil could see no trace of Christian customs or morality, and he felt that the Kiatagmiut needed primary instruction in the Catechism. It was not sufficient to make brief visits to the people once or twice a year to take their confession and give them communion. He gloomily reflected that it was a sin to give communion to unbelieving and unwilling people (DRHA, vol. 2, pp. 136-137).

> Often . . . when I call the people together, I get a reply that they are taking baths in a community hut, that they have gone to inspect the creels or that they are fishing: or they simply refuse to come. And if they say they will come, we have to wait hours until all of them have arrived. . . . One of them, who was sitting near the table on which were the cross and the gospel, asked for a vessel and urinated. . . . Very few listen: some of them sleep during my instructions, others go in and out, still others leave the community hut and do not return. . . . I still have patience but I do not have

any consolation of hope that the seed of God's Word will bear fruit in their hearts or even sprout (DRHA, vol. 1, p. 137).

Theophil further notes that many did not come to the Liturgy during his visits to the upriver villages, and many of those who did come refused communion, saying that they could not give up their shamanistic practices (DRHA, vol. 1, p. 138).

In order to obtain a better understanding of the Orthodox approach to the Eskimos of the Nushagak River region, it is suitable to mention here a series of instructions directed by Veniaminov, after he had become Metropolitan of Moscow, to Hieromonk Theophil at Nushagak. These instructions were, of course, meant to refer to relations between Orthodox missionaries and native peoples in all of Russian America. However, they were addressed to the Nushagak missionary by the man who, as a priest and later as bishop, took a special interest in the people of southwestern Alaska. Therefore, the following representative instructions are interesting not only in revealing official attitudes of the church, but in reflecting, perhaps, the Metropolitan's special interest in the Eskimos of the Nushagak River region.

1. Because of the nature of the country which makes it almost impossible for the inhabitants to observe the fasts in the usual manner, they should not be forced to observe the fasts by a change of diet.

2. Attendance at ordinary services should not be made an absolute duty.

3. With regard to the celebration of marriages, departures from the existing rules can be permitted only for the most cogent reasons and in cases of extreme necessity.

4. Ancient customs, as long as they are not contrary to Christianity, need not be too abruptly disturbed, but it should be explained to converts that these customs are merely tolerated.

5. No marriages entered into before baptism should be considered as hindrances to the administration of the Sacrament, nor should they be annulled.

6. Newly converted persons must not be given presents either before or after baptism nor should their sponsors be allowed to give them any.

7. No attempt should be made to increase the number of those

who receive baptism by compulsion, bribes or promises. The missionary shall at all times act with "apostolic sincerity."

8. Baptism shall not be administered to the Eskimos before they are thoroughly instructed and not even then unless they express a desire to receive it.

9. The missionary should not, upon arriving at a settlement, say he was sent by any government but should appear "in the guise of a poor wanderer, a sincere well-wisher to his fellowmen."

10. The missionary should strive to earn the good opinion of the people by the virtue and disinterestedness of his conduct.

11. On no account should the missionary show contempt for the customs of the people even though these customs may be deserving of it.

12. The missionary should do his best to earn the confidence of the people by wise kindliness and readiness to be of help in any way. "For who will open his heart to thee unless he trust thee?"

13. Those who show no desire to be baptized should not be coerced nor should the missionary be any less friendly toward them than toward the newly converted.

14. New converts should not be forced to make contributions to the church, but gifts may be accepted from those who voluntarily offer them provided that the use to which the gifts will be put is carefully explained so that they will not think that God demands offerings and sacrifices like their own idols.

15. The assistance of the Eskimos should be requested in a friendly manner, and guides and others offering help should be paid for their services.

16. The missionary should not, under any circumstances, enter into commercial transactions with the Eskimos.

17. Journeys should be undertaken at times when they will not interfere with the subsistence activities of the people, nor with the earnings of the Company.

18. The missionary and his assistant should become familiar with the native language as quickly as possible.

19. The missionary should find out all about the culture of his parishioners in order to influence them more easily.

20. Friendly advice for the improvement of their manner of

living may be offered to the people and this advice should be adapted to local conditions.

21. The missionary should not, under any circumstances, meddle in temporal affairs or attempt to discredit any of the authorities placed over the people either by the government or by themselves.

22. The missionary should keep a diary and this should be submitted to his superiors each year.

23. Whenever possible, a primary school should be started to instruct the children in the Catechism and reading.

These selected instructions reflect Veniaminov's knowledge of the Eskimos of Alaska and his willingness to allow flexibility in the application of the rules of the church. Quite likely flexible rules such as these, although probably not followed to the letter by all missionaries, accounted for the success which the Orthodox Church eventually achieved in the Nushagak River region.

In this regard it is interesting to note that by 1864, all the Eskimos in all the villages which the missionary was able to visit had been baptized (DRHA, vol. 1, p. 149). In 1866 a new church was built at Nushagak, although whether this was a completely new building or whether the one built in 1860 was simply enlarged and repaired is not clear (DRHA, vol. 1, p. 333). During the summer of that year, Theophil made a trip along the Kuskokwim River, perhaps because of the temporary absence of the priest for the Yukon district.

When Alaska was sold to the United States in 1867, the Orthodox Church immediately acted to reduce the number of clergymen and parishes in the new American territory. This move seems to have been prompted by a fear that it would be impossible for the Yukon and Nushagak parishes to exist after the removal of the Russian-American Company's posts and their Russian employes because of the difficulties involved in receiving food and church supplies and equipment. Consequently, Hieromonk Theophil left Nushagak on June 16, 1868. The mission was left in the care of Vasili E. Orlov, a mixed-blood, described by some sources as a lay reader and by others as first a sexton and then a deacon. At one time or another he may have occupied all these positions.

Orlov, who had begun his long service to the Nushagak mission in 1860, was to be paid $240 a year for the care of church property and for lay reader's duties (DRHA, vol. 1, pp. 152, 251).

Meanwhile, church membership in the Nushagak region continued to grow. An American observer, Charles Bryant, who visited Nushagak in 1868, mentions that out of a total population of 2,500 in the area, 1,800 had been baptized, registered in church records, and married in conformity with church regulations (Bryant and McIntyre, 1869, p. 23). In 1871, Orlov reported that the Nushagak mission "took care of" 2,080 people, 108 of whom were baptized that year. Although there was no priest, Orlov noted optimistically that "A number of people gather in one barabara each holiday to sing church songs and read: one person reads in Russian, the others listen and all of them understand what is being said. . . ." (DRHA, vol. 1, pp. 314-315). Although reports are conflicting, membership in the Nushagak church in 1878-1879 appears to have been close to 2,400, making it the second largest of the nine parishes in the diocese. Only the Yukon parish was larger, although the Kodiak parish was almost as large (DRHA, vol. 1, p. 116).

During the period between 1853 and 1878 there are no definite references in the available sources to Vasili Shishkin who came to Nushagak in 1842 and who is briefly mentioned by Veniaminov as being there in 1853 (Barsukov, 1897-1901, vol. 1, p. 407). Possibly Shishkin served the Nushagak mission continuously into the American period, but there are indications that he was on Kodiak Island, at least in 1860. He emerged from obscurity in 1878 and is referred to as a priest at Nushagak (Russian-American Company Records: Communications Sent, vol. 42, no. 445, folio 166). In his journal for that year he commented on the poor condition of the physical plant: a new roof was needed for the church, a new parish house was needed, and all church buildings badly required repairs and paint. Father Shishkin also makes the first reference to chapels in the Nushagak region supported by the parishioners themselves. There were six of these and in 1878 their members made donations totaling $24.10. The location of these chapels is not given but it is likely that there was one at Togiak, perhaps at Igushik and on the Alaska Peninsula, and at least one up the Nushagak River. Comments concerning relations between baptized and unbaptized Eskimos in the area are interesting. Father Shishkin says that the baptized people call the unbaptized ones dogs and consider it offensive to eat with them from the same vessel (DRHA, vol. 1, pp. 329, 331, 333).

The continued presence of Father Shishkin at Nushagak together with a visit to the area in 1878 by Innokentii Shavashnikov, a priest at Unalaska, seems to suggest that the church authorities overcame their fears about the continued existence of the northern missions after the purchase of Alaska by the United States. An American firm replaced the Russian-American Company at both St. Michael and Nushagak and indications reveal that church personnel were able to trade with the Americans and also ship and receive supplies through them while maintaining relations that were, at least in Nushagak, friendly. Father Shishkin mentioned that all church money at Nushagak in 1878 was kept in the safe of the Alaska Commercial Company (DRHA, vol. 1, p. 333).

Shavashnikov's travels included a visit to the Kuskokwim, Nushagak, and Ugashik regions, and to St. Michael. He reported that he was enthusiastically greeted by the Eskimos but they complained about the infrequency of missionary visits. The priest quoted the Eskimos as saying:

> Russian priests baptized us, they taught us about God and Jesus Christ, for which we are and shall always be grateful. But why did they desert us? Did we offend them? Now the savages (they call their own unbaptized peoples savages) laugh at us and say that the priests fooled us and deserted us; it is painful for us to hear that.

The Eskimos go on to refer to their chapels as being "worse than barns," filled with rubbish and attracting only dogs. These circumstances mainly applied to the Kuskokwim River, but Shavashnikov obviously was concerned about the general condition of the northern regions and he recommended the appointment of three additional missionaries for the area (DRHA, vol. 1, p. 155).

The relatively restricted influence of the missionaries in the Nushagak River region and the weak hold of Christianity on the minds of the Eskimo population at this time was also noted by Ivan Petroff. He stated that although all the Eskimos were carried on the register of the Orthodox church, rarely did the outlying settlements receive even an annual visit from the missionary and consequently his influence did not extend much beyond the baptism of infants and the marriage of the couples who visited the mission (Petroff, 1884, pp. 135-136).

At this time, however, Father Shishkin appears to have been making at least yearly trips up the Nushagak River and to other areas within his district. In his journal for December 27, 1881, he wrote:

> After the service for a safe journey, churchman (Vasili) Orlov, five laborers and I went up the Nushagak River in two dog sleds to preach to and baptize the savages and to satisfy the religious needs of Christians living in the villages of Kakuak, Agivavik, Kaliganek and Mulchatna. [On] January 2, 1882 we arrived at the village of Kakuak and began to hold services, to preach and to baptize the babies. In the evening we celebrated vespers and took confessions of those who wished to partake of the Holy Communion of Epiphany Day [January 19]. The total number of communicants together with the newly baptized was 154. . . .

They followed the same procedure at the other villages and this particular trip took sixty days (DRHA, vol. 2, p. 144). Beginning in January, 1883, Father Shishkin and Orlov traveled up the Nushagak, across to the Naknek River, up the Kvichak River to Iliamna Lake, over to Cook Inlet and back, across the divide to the Mulchatna, and down the Nushagak River (see map 2). This trip lasted eighty-five days. During the summer of the same year they made extensive trips to Togiak and Igushik (DRHA, vol. 2, pp. 145-146).

In evaluating his work during this period Father Shishkin considered the moral condition of the local Eskimos to be good as the people had practically discarded their pagan customs. However, the Nushagak and Kuskokwim, living as they did far from the church, retained many of their old beliefs and practices. He saw little hope of any improvement until these people could be visited more frequently—at least two times a year. The priest recommended that a second missionary be appointed for this large area and also readers named for the various chapels to hold services at Nushagak when the priest was away. All this would suggest that the Kuskokwim River was once considered to be more in the territory of the Nushagak missionary district than in that of the Yukon. The appropriation of a special salary of at least $60.00 a year for the readers was recommended as the villages were too poor to support them (DRHA, vol. 2, p. 144).

Father Shishkin makes a comment that is prophetic with regard to changes that were soon to take place in the religious orientation of the Nushagak River region. In the early summer of 1884 he met "two heterodox missionaries" who visited Nushagak and who later that same summer made a trip up to Kuskokwim River. These were the Moravian missionaries William H. Weinland and Henry Hartmann who were looking for a place to establish their mission. Father Shishkin, realizing how thinly represented the Orthodox Church was in the vast area north and west of Nushagak, recommended the establishment of "our own missionary quarters on the Kuskokwim River with a priest and two song leaders." He urged haste and even recommended that Vasili Orlov, described as the deacon at Nushagak, take over the Kuskokwim operation; ". . . otherwise orthodox Christianity will be smothered by heterodox missionaries" (DRHA, vol. 2, pp. 146-147). Father Shishkin's fear of "heterodox missionaries" was not a product of his imagination but had a basis in fact. The era during which the Russian Orthodox Church had a clear field in Alaska was rapidly drawing to a close.

In the summer of 1884, in response to an appeal from Dr. Sheldon Jackson, a Presbyterian minister and also a special federal agent for education in Alaska, the Moravian Church sent Hartmann and Weinland to southwestern Alaska in search of a suitable location at which to establish a mission. They proceeded from San Francisco to Unalaska and obtained passage on one of the small steamers belonging to the Alaska Commercial Company that made frequent trips to the mainland. The missionaries arrived at Nushagak on June 2, 1884, where they met John W. Clark, agent of the Alaska Commercial Company, who introduced them to Father Shishkin.

> He was very friendly and communicative, and readily replied to all our questions. He claims the Nushagak and Togiak districts as his parish, and showed us that according to his books he had 2,476 communicants. The natives are required to express belief in the teaching of the Greek Church, the Holy Trinity, and in Christ as the Saviour of mankind. Then they are baptized and become com-

municant members. Their children are also baptized, and supposed to be afterwards taught. At our request he took us to the
church and showed and explained everything: . . . In the course
of conversation he suggested to us the Kuskokwim, as an unoccupied field. Our prayer to the Lord had frequently been that he
should direct us in the right way by the men and means he chose.
So we took it as coming from Him that the Greek priest pointed
out that river, and came to the conclusion to abandon all search
for a suitable locality in the districts occupied by the Greek
Church. We determined to explore the Kuskokwim as far up the
river as it was advisable, and on our return to see Good News Bay,
unless the Lord should direct us otherwise (Jackson, 1886, pp.
57-58).

Father Shishkin obviously suggested the Kuskokwim region to
the Moravian missionaries in order to get rid of them or at least
to ensure that they did not establish their mission on his doorstep.
He certainly had no intention of relinquishing the area to the
Moravians as his immediate recommendation that an Orthodox
priest be appointed for the Kuskokwim River shows (see Oswalt,
1963, p. 38). At any rate, Hartmann and Weinland did explore the
Kuskokwim and the following year a mission was established at
the present site of Bethel.

In Weinland's report to the home board of the Moravian
Church, in 1885 after he had returned from the survey, he recommended that an industrial school be opened at Nushagak, suggesting at the same time that this location would be a good base
for operations in the interior and an excellent point for mail service both to and from the States. Those in charge of the Bethel
mission also realized early that communication between the station and the outside world would be much more frequent if there
was also an establishment at the mouth of the Nushagak River
where five salmon canneries were already located and where sailing vessels called several times during the year. Accordingly, in
the summer of 1886 the Rev. Mr. Frank E. Wolff of Green Bay,
Wisconsin, who had volunteered, sailed from San Francisco to
the mouth of the Nushagak for the purpose of setting up a building for the new mission and school (Schwalbe, 1951, p. 9; Hamilton, 1890, p. 10; 1892, p. 353).

Early in 1886, prior to the Rev. Mr. Wolff's trip to Nushagak,
the president of the Society of the United Brethren went to

Washington for an interview with the head of the Department of Education, the result of which was the signing of a contract with the government for a $1,500 grant to the Moravian Church to establish and conduct an industrial school at Nushagak. Wolff left Bethlehem for San Francisco on May 6 with instructions to obtain lumber for a house, schoolhouse, and woodshed and to have as much of the carpenter work as possible done in that city before leaving for Alaska. On August 21, he arrived at the cannery of the Arctic Packing Company near the Eskimo village of Kanulik. This village was located on the east side of Nushagak Bay approximately three miles north of Nushagak. Thirteen days after landing, Wolff, with the aid of men from the cannery, had completed the buildings and on the eighth of September, before returning to the States, he gave the key to a local Eskimo leader (SPG Proceedings, 1886, pp. 4-5, 23; Hamilton, 1892, p. 353; Schwalbe, 1951, pp. 51-52).

In the early summer of 1887 the Rev. Mr. Wolff, his wife and two children, and Miss Mary Huber of Lititz, Pennsylvania, sailed for the Nushagak River to open the new school and mission which was named Carmel. Thus the worst fears of the Orthodox priest were realized. At the beginning the Moravians emphasized their school activities at Carmel, perhaps realizing that they had, after all, assured Father Shishkin that they would carry on their missionary activities in a region at the periphery of Orthodox influence. The fact that they were now establishing a station right next to the long established Orthodox mission could not fail to antagonize the priest. As a result, relations between the two missions were strained and unpleasant from the beginning.

During the first summer the Moravians spent a great deal of time on preparations. The interiors of the hastily constructed buildings had to be insulated against the severe winter weather. By the first of January, 1888, the missionaries were ready to open their school and begin work. However, this was the time of the holiday festivities of the Orthodox Church and the entire population of Kanulik went to Nushagak to attend them and remained a week. Then native dances and festivities followed and not until January 17 was school able to begin. The Moravian school at Carmel, which was always to be an integral part of the mission activities in the Nushagak region, will be discussed in detail later. It may be noted here that the efforts of the Moravians both in education and active proselytizing were subject at all times to the opposition of the priest at Nushagak (Report of the Commissioner of Education. . . . 1887-1888, pub. 1889, p. 186; SPG Proceedings, 1888, p. 27).

In the summer of 1888 the Rev. John H. Schoechert of Watertown, Wisconsin joined the staff at Carmel as did Miss Emma Huber, sister of Mary Huber. She seems to have come after Mr. Schoechert, perhaps the following summer, and was hired as a teacher. Meanwhile the mission was expanding its activities and special services were held for the many salmon cannery workers in the Nushagak Bay region. This expansion did not take place without opposition from the Orthodox mission at Nushagak. The Carmel missionaries recorded that Deacon Orlov's wife was able to persuade Eskimo women not to work at Carmel, and the Moravians believed that several families had been induced to move from Kanulik in order to be away from the temptation to attend services at the mission (SPG Proceedings, 1888, p. 30). The journal of the missionaries for 1888 contains some of the first impressions the Moravians obtained of their Orthdox colleagues. One entry states that the Eskimos

> hold most devotedly to the Greek Church, of which they are, literally speaking, perfect slaves; nearly every hut has a picture of Alexander the Great [sic], before which the natives bow and cross themselves. About the priest I will refrain from saying more than that he is a drunkard, gambler. . . . He travels all over the country and warns the people against our school; and is often so sadly intoxicated that he cannot keep the appointed service, even after the natives have traveled for many miles in order to attend. Yet he holds a great influence over these poor deluded beings, who sometimes seem to be at a loss to know what to think about the present state of affairs. They sometimes seem to think that their old priest is not just what he should be; but he has been amongst them so long a time that they can understand and talk freely with him (SPG Proceedings, 1888, p. 31).

On June 30, 1888, the missionaries at Carmel were surprised to receive a visit from A. P. Swineford, governor of Alaska, who was making a tour of inspection. During his stay he appointed Mr. Clark, of the Alaska Commercial Company, as justice of the peace and Mr. Louis Guenther, caretaker of the cannery at Kanulik, constable. The latter appointment seems to have been at least partly in response to complaints by the Moravians that territorial school laws could not be enforced because of the strong Orthodox objections to the Moravian school (SPG Proceedings, 1888, p. 61).

The Rev. John H. Kilbuck of the Moravian mission at Bethel visited Carmel during the winter of 1889 after an arduous trip by dog team from the Kuskokwim. His visit encouraged Kilbuck's colleagues, who were finding Father Shishkin's opposition very demoralizing. On Thanksgiving Day, 1888, a special dinner had been arranged for the students at the Moravian school but the priest ordered them not to attend; the same thing happened to a special entertainment that had been prepared for Christmas. Kilbuck's ability to speak the Eskimo language was a particular marvel and stimulus to the Carmel missionaries (Hamilton, 1892, pp. 355-356; 1890, p. 18).

During part of 1889 and 1890 Father Shishkin seems to have been absent from the Nushagak mission on a visit to San Francisco and during his absence the Carmel missionaries enjoyed a respite from what they considered his persecution. During this period the Moravians felt that they had made some progress in their ministrations to the men of the various canneries and, in addition, two female students of the school were candidates for membership in the church. Sixteen adults, nine of them Eskimos, were also listed as members by the end of 1890 (Hamilton, 1890, p. 19; Schwalbe, 1951, p. 59). Nevertheless, the missionaries in their report for 1890-1891 ruefully recalled the treatment meted out to Eskimos who attended services at Carmel: they were forced to confess their attendance to the priest and then he punished them by making them kneel before him on salt, bowing all the time (SPG, Proceedings, 1891, p. 28). In spite of these and other problems the authorities in Bethlehem must have been reasonably impressed with the success, or at least the promise, of the Carmel mission because Mr. Wolff's request for 30,000 feet of prepared lumber to build a larger schoolhouse and a chapel was approved and the material was shipped from San Francisco in the summer of 1890 (Hamilton, 1890, p. 30). In the summer of 1891, Bishop Henry T. Bachman of the Moravian Church visited Alaska for the first time. He seems to have been impressed with the development of the mission at Bethel, but had strangely little to say about Carmel except that he believed the hope of this mission lay in the development of the school rather than in specifically religious activities (SPG Proceedings, 1891, pp. 77-78).

Meanwhile, the Russian Orthodox Church seems to have been maintaining and even extending its influence in the region. In their report on conditions in the territory, the enumerators of the Eleventh Census noted that the influence of the Orthodox Church at Nushagak was so extensive that it could be looked upon as the established church of the region. Nearly all the coast Eskimos of the area were members and Father Shishkin had been successful in training lay readers to conduct services in some of the outlying villages. The priest, in spite of his advanced age, made regular trips throughout his parish during which he might be absent from the mission for as long as two months and cover from three hundred to eight hundred miles. On these trips he baptized the children, married young couples and ratified the marriages that had already been consummated, and gave the last blessing to those who had died since his previous visit. He sold candles and pictures of saints to help recover the expenses for these trips. The enumerators further noted that the Orthodox Church, although it was the only remaining institution that went back to the period of Russian occupation, exerted so strong an influence upon its Eskimo members that some of them were not even aware that the territory had been transferred to United States ownership. The Eskimos were said to divide all mankind into two classes, Russians and non-Russians. Anyone who was unable to speak Russian was looked upon as pitifully ignorant and treated with contempt (Porter, 1893, p. 96).

Father Shishkin's long period of service at Nushagak ended in 1893-1894 when he died and was buried in the cemetery on the hill behind the village. He had served the mission either continuously, or nearly so, for more than fifty years, and was replaced by Father Vladimir V. Modestov (DRHA, vol. 1, p. 244).

In 1894 the Rev. Mr. Wolff and his family left the Moravian mission and two years later the Rev. Mr. Samuel Rock joined the group at Carmel. In 1897 Rock married the schoolteacher, Emma Huber. An important mission activity during 1894 and 1895 was the formation of a temperance society. In this connection nearly all the fishermen and other whites in the Nushagak Bay area signed a paper promising to aid and support mission efforts to prevent the Eskimos from making intoxicants. Apparently the members of this society had regular meetings, elected a "lookout committee," and struck from membership those individuals who backslid. Most members appear to have been cannery workers, but some Eskimos were involved (Schwalbe, 1951, p. 57; Alaska Records, 1892-1938, p. 16; Report of the Commissioner of Education. . . . 1894-1895, pub. 1896, vol. 2, p. 1430).

The Moravian sources, both published and archival, contain no reference to trips up the Nushagak River until 1895-1896 when eight trips appear to have been made, at least one of which was to Togiak. Quite probably both Mr. Schoechert and Mr. Rock took part in these trips (SPG Proceedings, 1896, pp. 27-28). Although many children were presumably baptized, the first adult communicant from upriver did not become a member of the church until April, 1896. This was a man who was given the name Abraham Grant and who was to act as a lay reader, or "helper" (Alaska Material, box vi, Records of Ecclesiastical Acts, No. 3). In early January of 1896, the missionaries traveled up the Nushagak to Kokwok, a large village about one hundred miles from the Carmel mission. They were well received and talked to the people in the *kashgee,* or ceremonial house. The missionaries were told that the Orthodox priest, on an earlier trip to the village, had warned the people against the Moravians who would teach them the ways of the devil (Alaska Records, 1892-1938, pp. 40-42). Baptisms are not mentioned in the records and the missionaries seem to have confined their activities to preaching, through an interpreter, and to the singing of hymns.

Sometime in 1896, presumably after he became a member of the church in April, Abraham Grant was sent up the Nushagak as a "helper" to preach to the upriver people. He established himself at a place which the Moravians always refered to as "Grant's Village," located approximately nine miles below Kokwok on the west bank of the river. Mr. Schoechert made a trip to Grant's Village in September of that year and work was begun on a small chapel that was finished the following year. In October of 1896 a trip was made up the Wood River, probably the first penetration by the Moravians into this area. Four villages were visited and the reception accorded the missionaries was friendly. In January of 1897 Mr. Schoechert baptized 13 individuals at Kokwok and Grant's Village, the first recorded upriver baptisms (SPG Proceedings, 1897, p. 23; Alaska Material, box vi, Records of Ecclesiastical Acts, No. 3). The missionaries stepped up their activities on the Nushagak River in 1897-1898, and made four visits to Grant's Village and Kokwok. A chapel was under construction in the latter village and it was planned to send a native helper from Kanulik and his wife to live there (SPG Proceedings, 1898, p. 25).

Father Modestov departed Nushagak in 1897 or 1898 and the Orthodox mission was left in the charge of Deacon Vasili P. Kashevarov who had apparently begun his service in 1896 (DRHA, vol. 1, pp. 225-226). The Moravians reported a steady growth of interest in their work among Eskimos on the Nushagak and they began to turn their attention to the Togiak River region. Because the Moravians considered the salmon canneries in the bay area as a bad influence on the Eskimos, they urged their people to remain upriver during the summer months and, consequently, attempted to visit the stations at Kokwok and Grant's Village as frequently as possible. No evidence indicates that they were successful in their efforts to stem the annual movement of Nushagak people to the coast during the summer (Report of the Commissioner of Education . . . 1898-1899, pub. 1900, vol. 2, p. 1395; SPG Proceedings, 1900, p. 45).

During the winter of 1899-1900 Schoechert and Rock collected the census data to be incorporated in the Twelfth United States Census. Schoechert appears to have gone to Togiak and also inland, while Rock covered the Alaska Peninsula as far as Katmai. Church membership was found to have increased greatly by 1900, with 211 members in contrast to 18 in 1890 (SPG Proceedings, 1900, p. 46; Schwalbe, 1951, p. 58).

In 1899 Mary Huber went on leave but she seems to have returned to Carmel after slightly more than a year. The Schoecherts departed in or about 1902 and were replaced by Mr. and Mrs. Paul Zucher. Mr. Zucher was made station superintendent while Mr. Rock became missionary in charge (Schwalbe, 1951, p. 60). The annual report of the missionaries for 1901 describes an Easter service at Carmel:

> About 4 a.m. both bells were rung, which soon brought the natives together, the men filling the boys' room of the schoolhouse and the

women coming into our kitchen. All were served with a cup of hot tea. The next bell called us together in our schoolroom and chapel, where the morning service was opened in the usual way. Part of the scripture was read in English and part in the native language. Then we went to the cemetary, . . . Although there was a sharp, cold wind blowing, and the morning cloudy, yet everyone seemed pleased to remember the resurrection of Christ while standing among the graves of the departed ones (Report of the Commissioner of Education. . . . 1901, pub. 1902, vol. 2, pp. 1476-1477).

At the close of 1903, the Carmel mission was in the charge of the Rev. Mr. Paul Zucher and in the summer of 1904 Mr. and Mrs. Rock went to the United States on furlough. During that summer Dr. J. H. Romig and his wife, formerly of the Bethel mission and returning to Alaska after a furlough in the States, came to Carmel to assist the Zuchers. Dr. Romig has been authorized to establish a hospital and general medical practice at Nushagak as an adjunct to the mission. He hoped to maintain a small hospital in the mission buildings from which he could serve not only the Eskimos but also cannery employes. He was also expected to make an effort to do evangelistic work among these same cannery employes and thus enlarge the sphere of the mission as a center of Christian influence (Schwalbe, 1951, p. 61; Report of the Commissioner of Education. . . . 1903, pub. 1905, vol. 2, p. 2358).

During the summer of 1905 Bishop J. Taylor Hamilton visited the Moravian missions in Alaska as a representative of the Mission Board. Stopping first at Carmel, he held a conference with the Romig and Zucher families. The bishop was informed that the church membership was "morally weak with but little comprehension of what is expected in the life of a real Christian" (Schwalbe, 1951, p. 61). At the same time he learned that Dr. Romig's experiment in medical missionary work was not the success that had originally been hoped for and that the doctor wished to discontinue this service. There was some talk of moving the mission buildings to "New Kanakanak" (present-day Kanakanak) where they would be easily accessible to residents of the Eskimo villages of Kanakanak and Chogiung (present-day Dillingham) but Bishop Hamilton thought the expense would be excessive (Hamilton, 1906, pp. 36, 39). He also recognized the hindrances to the work of the mission caused by the proximity of the Orthodox mission at Nushagak. "Unless the heart's conviction has brought an Eskimo into our communion, he has every incentive to resent reproof and baffle admonition and thwart discipline, with the declaration 'I am going over to the Greek Church'" (Hamilton, 1906, p. 32).

The canneries, with their large number of seasonal employes, most of them Oriental, seriously counteracted the efforts of the Moravian missionaries at Carmel. The Eskimos constantly loitered about the canneries whether they received employment or not; and in the eyes of the bishop and his colleagues, bad habits and new vices were acquired which made it virtually impossible for the missionaries to emphasize the importance of Christian standards. The cannery employes also taught the Eskimos to manufacture intoxicants and cases of church discipline were frequently connected with drinking (Hamilton, 1906, p. 33).

In July Bishop Hamilton moved to Bethel together with the Carmel missionaries where, from the twenty-sixth to the twenty-ninth of the month, the General Missionary Conference was held. The most important recommendation of this conference was that the missionary activity in Alaska be concentrated on the more important and promising Kuskokwim region and that the missionaries at Carmel be transferred to Bethel, the few faithful church members on the Nushagak also being encouraged to migrate to the more northern community. The general conclusion was that the Eskimos of the Nushagak River region were difficult to reach with the message of Christ's love. The language barrier was mentioned and also the "diffidence" and "innate reserve" of the Eskimo that caused him to resent intrusion into his private affairs (Schwalbe, 1951, pp. 63-64; SPG Proceedings, 1906, pp. 82-83).

The withdrawal from Carmel took place at the end of July, 1906. Zucher closed the mission buildings and, with his family, moved to Bethel. Although apparently a few Eskimos had agreed to migrate to the Kuskokwim, when the time came they had all changed their minds and few even were on hand to say good-bye to the departing missionary (Schwalbe, 1951, pp. 63-64; SPG Proceedings, 1906, pp. 70-75). A minute adopted at a meeting of the Board of Directors of the Society for Propagating the Gospel on October 24, 1905, at Bethlehem accurately sums up the official reasons for the demise of the Carmel mission. It is quoted here in part.

In view of the lamentable paucity of results of the missionary work on the Nushagak; of the gradual dying out of the natives; of the many practical difficulties connected with carrying on the work on the Nushagak; of the fact that apparently we have no men now in the field capable of coping with the situation; of the fact that the Togiak region can be better reached from Quinhagak than from Carmel—much as we regret to withdraw gospel privileges from any field which we have entered—we feel constrained regretfully to recommend to the Mission Board 1) that the Carmel Mission be transferred to the Kuskokwim, . . . 2) that henceforth efforts be concentrated on the Kuskokwim District, where more natives are within reach and where the outlook is encouraging (Alaska Material, box v, letters, box ii, folder 1, no. 5).

And so the Moravian mission on the Nushagak River came to an end. The reasons for its failure have been mentioned and are well summed up by the above quotation. The minute of the Board of Directors suggests, however, that personnel problems were more at the root of the mission's collapse than any external factors. Perhaps the Bethel mission might have suffered a similar fate had it not been for the vigorous leadership of John Kilbuck in the difficult early years. At any rate, the Moravians probably can not be thought of as having exerted a great deal of influence on the people of the Nushagak River region. Their sphere of operations was limited and they never succeeded in opening any new part of the region to outside influences. They entered the region in response to a certain set of circumstances, and their departure, after only twenty years, was an admission of their failure to be able to alter these circumstances. With regard to the Nushagak River itself, probably at no time did the influence of the Moravians extend beyond the community of Kokwok. All but a very small number of the total number of Moravian upriver baptisms took place at this community and at Grant's Village. Even at Kokwok, which must have had at this time a population approaching 150, there were only 30 members of the small log chapel in 1905 (Hamilton, 1906, p. 34). As far as the bay region is concerned, it is not difficult to imagine that, with the strong influence of the Orthodox Church and the secular atmosphere fostered by the canneries, the closing of the Carmel mission caused scarcely a ripple of interest among the permanent and seasonal residents.

Following the departure of the Moravians, the Orthodox

Church not only maintained its influence over the people of the region, but took back into the fold most of those who had been receptive to Moravian preaching. Vasili P. Kashevarov, who came to Nushagak in 1896, appears to have been replaced in 1900 by his brother Nicholas. At that time the church supported chapels at Ekuk, Paugvik at the mouth of the Naknek River, Iliamna, and Kakhonak on Iliamna Lake, and Semenovsky on Naknek Lake (DRHA, vol. 5, p. 61). Vasili returned in 1906 and remained at Nushagak where he died on June 29, 1916 (DRHA, vol. 1, pp. 223, 25-226). Under his leadership the Nushagak church maintained its influence even though the east side of the bay was slowly depopulated as large settlements grew up on the west side. After Father Kashevarov's death there was no priest at Nushagak for a long time and although other priests eventually served the community for brief periods, the church began a decline from which it never recovered. By 1916 an Orthodox Church had been established at Wood River Village near the mouth of that river, and later it served the growing Dillingham area. At Nushagak in recent years a lay reader conducted services and largely through the strength of his character maintained the influence on the Nushagak church until his death in 1963. Even when the village was nearly abandoned, people continued to cross the bay for services, particularly at Easter. The present priest at Dillingham, a son-in-law of the old Nushagak lay reader, wished to move the icons and other church equipment to the Dillingham church but his father-in-law objected strongly and the transfer was not accomplished until after the old man's death. Today the Nushagak church of St. Peter and St. Paul is locked and no longer used. The building itself is about thirty-five years old.

In the past three decades a number of churches have been established in the Nushagak region, notably the Seventh Day Adventists who founded a colony at the east end of Lake Aleknagik in 1930. This denomination now has a church in Dillingham as do the Roman Catholics, Church of Christ members, and Baptists. The Moravians entered the area again in 1954 and now have three churches in the general region. However, none of these other denominations has penetrated the interior to any great extent. The Russian Orthodox Church still claims the vast majority of the inhabitants of the Nushagak River as members.

III

Traders

◆◆◆

THE HISTORY OF TRADING ACTIVITY IN THE NUSHAGAK RIVER REGION IS closely linked with the early exploration of the area since this exploration was never motivated by a desire for increased geographical knowledge alone, but invariably was connected with the needs and demands of the fur trade. The Russian-American Company may have turned its attention to the vast unknown region north of the Alaska Peninsula because attempts to establish a foothold in California and the Hawaiian Islands were being thwarted. Also, by 1818 the supply of fur-bearing animals in the Aleutian Islands and southeastern Alaska had begun to diminish noticeably and the Company had to seek out new regions into which to expand its quest for furs. That other political factors were also responsible cannot be denied. The Russians during this period certainly had a vested interest in extending and strengthening their claim to areas of Alaska other than those where they had traditionally operated.

All these factors may have been in Baranov's mind when, as one of his last acts as general manager of the Company, he sent Korsakovski and his companions to found a trading post at the mouth of the Nushagak River in 1818. Fedor Kolmakov, the first manager of Alexandrovski Redoubt, had established trade relations with the neighboring Eskimos and generally helped to spread the Company's influence in this region. Kolmakov was apparently an energetic trader and Khromchenko, when he stopped at Alexandrovski Redoubt in the late spring of 1822, learned that

49

the manager was at that time at the mouth of the Togiak River
trading with the Eskimos for furs. While anchored at Hagemeister Island, Khromchenko met Eskimos who were accustomed to
dealing with Kolmakov and when these people came on board the
ship, they asked for snuff (Khromchenko, 1824, pt. 10, pp. 275,
306). Both Etolin and Khromchenko were very enthusiastic about
the potentialities of this newly opened region (Russian-American
Company Records: Communications Received, vol. 6, no. 346,
folio 102).

Yanovski's objections to the location of Alexandrovski Redoubt
reflected the Company's interest in locating a post in a region
that would be convenient for the native peoples of a large surrounding area and where supplies could be easily brought in and
furs shipped out. Alexandrovski Redoubt fulfilled these conditions
admirably at the time it was established and for a number of
years thereafter (DRHA, vol. 2, pp. 243-244). In fact, as early as
1828 Kolmakov made an annual shipment of more than 4,000
beaver and otter pelts from the post (Russian-American Company
Records: Communications Sent, vol. 6, no. 114, folio 82). In the
fall of 1829 he invited the peoples of the Kuskokwim River to
come to Alexandrovski and during the winter more than 200 men
came to Lake Aleknagik where Kolmakov traded with them (Russian-American Company Records: Communications Sent, vol. 7,
no. 257, folio 272).

Vasiliev's explorations in 1829 and 1830 were carried out mainly for the purpose of establishing trade relations with the natives.
However, when F. P. Wrangell visited Alexandrovski during the
summer of 1832 he was dissatisfied with the extent to which Eskimos from the interior regions visited the redoubt to trade. Therefore, he proposed to send a hunting detachment to the interior
that would winter on the Kuskokwim River and return to the redoubt in the spring. In order to encourage this detachment to
trade with the Kuskokwim Eskimos and not with those closer to
the post, Wrangell offered a reward consisting of one-fortieth
part of the value of the furs for pelts brought from the distant
river. Fedor Kolmakov was named leader of this detachment.
When the party returned after being absent from Alexandrovski

for seven months, they brought with them 1,150 beaver and otter pelts. The following summer Kolmakov and Lukin again visited the Kuskokwim, the former returning to the redoubt in Feburary, 1834, with 1,002 pelts while Lukin wintered at the mouth of the Kwik River (Russian-American Company Records: Communications Sent, vol. 9, no. 321, folios 482-487; no. 460, folios 347-348; vol. 11, no. 73, folios 95-97; no. 272, folio 252).

These efforts of Wrangell, Kolmakov, and Lukin to widen the sphere of influence of Alexandrovski Redoubt were highly successful. By the time of Zagoskin's interior explorations of 1842-1844, communications between Kolmakovski Redoubt on the Kuskokwim River and Alexandrovski were frequent. In winter it was customary for a transport of furs containing from ten to fifteen sleds, accompanied by as many as fifteen dog drivers and guides, to leave the Kuskokwim post around the middle of February and make its way up the Holokuk River from the headwaters of which there was a long portage to the upper Holitna River. Here the transport rested and took on additional supplies that were cached in this area during the summer months. From this point the transport would proceed overland, probably following a small tributary of the Holitna known today as Shotgun Creek. Then the sleds would presumably pass overland to the upper Nushagak where a stop would be made at the Nushagak *odinochka* or trail house, where more supplies could be obtained along with fresh dogs and new drivers and guides. Zagoskin says that the *odinochka* consisted of one building (*izba*), probably a traditional Eskimo house, occupied by two Russian watchmen and sometimes a number of Aglegmiut Eskimos. From the trail house the transports would proceed down the Nushagak River to Alexandrovski Redoubt. This route was difficult and might require four to five weeks or even longer to traverse.

In summer a convoy of one-, two-, and three-hatch baidarki would make its way up the Kuskokwim from Kolmakovski Redoubt and then up the Holitna and one of the Holitna's upper tributaries. When necessary the cargo and boats would be portaged overland. Presumably a portage would be necessary only at the divide between the Kuskokwim and Nushagak drainages. Zagoskin says that this was a distance of about seven miles. At the Nushagak *odinochka,* rafts would be built and the furs loaded on them for the trip to Alexandrovski Redoubt. The Eskimos with their baidarki would be discharged and presumably would return to the Kuskokwim. Frequently in summer supplies were brought up the Nushagak to the *odinochka* where the supply detachment met a fur convoy coming from the Kuskokwim. Then the furs would be loaded for the trip to Alexandrovski and the supplies ferried by baidarki to Kolmakovski Redoubt (Zagoskin, 1956, pp. 261-262).

It is not known exactly when the Nushagak *odinochka* was constructed, but it appears to have been in use by 1835 (Russian-American Company Records: Communications Sent, vol. 12, no. 256, folios 152-153). Its major function was almost certainly as described above: to provide a resting place and trans-shipment point on the route between the two redoubts. The exact location of this trail house is also uncertain, although the approximate locality can be determined. On the Zagoskin (1956) and Glazunov (VanStone, 1959, p. 38) maps the site is shown on the east bank of the river well above the mouth of the Nuyakuk River. This stretch of the upper Nushagak was called the Ilgayak River by Zagoskin and on the Glazunov map is called the Ilgajack; thus it is likely that the *odinochka* was located at or near the mouth of what is today called the King Salmon River. Because of the unstable nature of the riverbanks in this region, it is doubtful whether the exact site could be determined today. Also, as previously mentioned, the remains of the trail house, if discovered, would probably not differ markedly from the traditional Eskimo dwelling of the region.

Alexandrovski Redoubt's importance as a center of the fur trade north of the Alaska Peninsula did not last long. In 1833 F. P. Wrangell, then general manager of the Company, ordered the construction of Mikhailovski Redoubt; and this new post served as a base not only for explorations into the Yukon country, but also for the shipment of furs from this previously untapped region. At the same time, Nikolaevski Redoubt on Cook Inlet, founded much earlier in 1791, began to play a bigger part as a possible supply base and communication point for the newly opened interior of southwestern Alaska.

Fedor Kolmakov died on August 20, 1839, and was replaced as manager by his son Petr (Russian-American Company Records: Communications Sent, vol. 17, no. 509, folios 493-497). Apparently the younger Kolmakov, although an experienced explorer, lacked the administrative abilities of his father and in the winter of 1842 was replaced by a Mr. Volkov who had been manager of the redoubt on Atka (Russian-American Company Records: Communications Sent, vol. 21, no. 35, folios 31-32). In the previous year, the manager of the Kodiak office visited Alexandrovski to settle a dispute about the prices paid for furs. His orders from the general manager reveal some interesting details about the fur trade. He was instructed not to raise the prices paid in tobacco, beads, cloth, and other so-called luxury items used by the Eskimos. On the other hand, if the payments were to be made in blankets, heavy cloth, canvas tent cloth, and other materials that could be used for garments, then the price could be raised. The reasoning here was that if the Eskimos were expected to trade all their furs, then they must be given a favorable opportunity to acquire other materials with which to clothe themselves. Suggested prices that the Kodiak manager might put into effect at the redoubt were as follows:

> Four large, spread out beaver or otter pelts are equal to a good woolen blanket included in the Company's capital at from fifteen to twenty rubles; one large beaver is equal to four arshins of Romanov canvas or calico; one large beaver is equal to four arshins of tent cloth; one large beaver is equal to two or three skins of wild goats (if they prove suitable for the natives).

A final instruction to the Kodiak manager was that the Eskimos should be encouraged, "with gifts and kind words," to hunt beavers under the ice in winter when the pelts were in prime condition rather than after breakup when they were greatly reduced in value (Russian-American Company Records: Communications Sent, vol. 20, no. 43, folios 51-56).

In 1846, during Mikhail Dmitrievich Tebenkov's tenure as general manager of the Company, the decision was made to act on A. K. Etolin's recommendation and reduce Alexandrovski from a redoubt to an *odinochka* and subordinate it to the Nikolaevski Re-

doubt. The effects of this decision on the activities of the Orthodox Church have already been noted. The manager, Mr. Volkov,
and other unnecessary employes were transferred to Kodiak and
the post was put in the charge of a *baidarshchik* with two workers
and one interpreter (DRHA, vol. 1, pp. 365-366; Tikhmenev,
1939-1940, pt. II, p. 218; Russian-American Company Records:
Communications Sent, vol. 27, no. 267, folios 386-387). From that
time on, Alexandrovski is consistently referred to as an *odinochka*
in the Company's official correspondence although Tebenkov's
map of 1849 (1852) and Zagoskin's map (1956) designated it as
"fort" (*krepost*). In the vital statistics of the Nushagak church,
there is a reference to Nushagak *odinochka* (not the upriver trail
house) as early as 1847, but by 1879 the community is regularly
referred to as Alexandrovski Redoubt (Alaska Russian Church Archives, accession 12,766, vital statistics, Nushagak, 1842-1931). It
would seem that the old name continued without reference to the
reduced importance of the trading post.

From the records of the Russian-American Company may be
extracted some scanty information concerning the methods by
which the manager at Alexandrovski Redoubt dealt with the Eskimos of the surrounding area for furs. When new contacts with remote villages were made, for example, with the settlements on the
upper Nushagak and Kuskokwim rivers, the manager attempted
to determine the community leaders, or *toyons* as the Russians
called them. These individuals were given silver medals, called
"United Russia," with the Tsar's picture on one side, a certificate
designating the leader as a person of authority recognized by the
Company, and occasional incentive gifts. The general manager
frequently warned Kolmakov and his successors at Alexandrovski
against handing out the medals indiscriminately. The post manager was charged with keeping a careful account of those medals
he did distribute and even with trying to retrieve them from the
families of *toyons* who died so that they might be awarded once
again. The *toyons* were supposed to be individuals who were re-
spected by the people and whose friendly relations with the
Russians would be a definite benefit to the Company. They encouraged their fellow villagers to hunt and bring their furs to the
redoubt or to the *odinochka* associated with it. Probably the *toyons*
never wielded as much power and authority in their communities

as the Company's officials thought they did. Nevertheless, in one way or another, a faithful *toyon* could often encourage hunters in his village to expend more energy in the Company's behalf than they might otherwise have been inclined to do (Russian-American Company Records: Communications Sent, vol. 8, no. 322, folio 247; vol. 9, no. 460, folio 350; vol. 16, no. 467, folios 178-179; vol. 17, no. 387, folios 370-371; vol. 17, no. 388, folios 371-372).

Although this was the traditional manner of dealing for furs with inhabitants of southwestern Alaska, the Russians did not hesitate to try other methods if they gave promise of being successful. For example, in the summer of 1839 Petr Kolmakov went from Alexandrovski Redoubt with a party of hired Eskimos to hunt for beavers. The hunters were paid a specific wage and all furs taken belonged to the Company. This hunt was not only highly successful, but the Eskimos seemed to approve of the new arrangement (Russian-American Company Records: Communications Sent, vol. 18, no. 335, folios 314-317).

At the time of Tikhmenev's study of the Russian-American Company in the period around 1860, trading activities of the Company were divided into two administrative districts with headquarters at Kodiak and Sitka. The Kodiak district included Prince William Sound, Cook Inlet, the northern part of the Alaska Peninsula, the islands of the Kodiak archipelago, Bristol Bay, the Nushagak River, and the Kuskokwim River region. Tikhmenev tells us that at this time the Nushagak trading post was under the direction of a manager with about twenty employes, a surprisingly large number considering the extent to which the post had been reduced in 1846. The fur trade was conducted on a small scale and mostly with the neighboring Aglegmiut Eskimos. Tikhmenev conveys the definite impression that Alexandrovski was an insignificant post partly because the people of the region were careless and uninspired trappers and partly because other posts on Cook Inlet and on the Kuskokwim and Yukon rivers had siphoned away much of the trade. The most popular trade goods of the period were tobacco, various kinds of dry goods, and cast iron kettles. Beads, particularly large red, black and white ones, had formerly been much preferred by the Eskimos of the region, but these had fallen from favor and were bartered only in small quantities

(Tikhmenev, 1939-1940, pt. II, p. 334). Other goods bartered by the Russians in western Alaska which were likely to have been included in the Nushagak trading inventories were knives, iron spears, steel for striking a fire, needles, combs, pipes, cooking pots, large cups, mirrors, copper rings, earrings, bracelets of copper and iron, leather pouches, pestles and mortars, small bells, navy buttons, Aleutian axes, flannel blankets, and items of European clothing (Zagoskin, 1956, pp. 137, 153, 164, 252-253).

Although the method is not explicitly stated in the sources, we can assume that the Eskimos of this area, like those in other parts of Alaska, were encouraged to become indebted to the Company in order to insure that they would have to trade with or work for the local post. The more closely the Eskimos were bound to the Company and the more heavily they relied on the trader for supplies and items of European manufacture, the less likely they were to pursue traditional subsistence activities. Certainly many aboriginal hunting techniques began to be forgotten at this time. The Company assumed a paternal role, controlling the goods which the Eskimos could obtain and carefully regulating how much they were to receive. Aside from these generalities, however, no details are known of the actual mechanics of the fur trade at Alexandrovski Redoubt, the relations between traders and Eskimos, the formalities of the trading process, inventories of trade goods, or relative values of furs and trade goods.

The outline presented above serves to indicate that the Alexandrovski Redoubt, after an initial short period of importance as the only Company post north of the Alaska Peninsula, lapsed into relative obscurity with the emergence of other posts and the establishment of better lines of communication throughout the entire region of southwestern Alaska. In fact, as early as 1851 the Company would have liked to close the Nushagak post altogether because of difficulties between the *baidarshchik* and the Eskimos, and because of the small amount of fur being shipped from there. They hesitated to do this, however, because of the mission, even though no priest was in residence at the time. When Hieromonk Theophil was sent to Nushagak in 1853 it then became impossible to abolish the *odinochka* (Russian-American Company Records:

Communications Sent, vol. 32, no. 278, folios 132-133; vol. 34, no. 382, folio 130).

Perhaps the most significant point to emerge from the history of Alexandrovski Redoubt is the manner in which it illustrates how rapidly the Eskimos of southwestern Alaska were exposed to the fur trade. Between 1818 and 1840 the entire region was opened and trading contacts were established throughout the heavily populated Yukon and Kuskokwim river systems as well as along the Nushagak.

In 1867 Hutchison, Kohl and Company of San Francisco purchased the assets of the Russian-American Company. This company, which apparently operated the Nushagak post for at least one year and possibly two, was soon reorganized to form the Alaska Commercial Company which dominated trade in southwestern Alaska throughout the rest of the nineteenth century and well into the twentieth. With the beginning of the American period of influence in the Nushagak River region, information concerning the fur trade and other economic activities is more bountiful. This is certainly owing to the greatly increased number of visitors to the area and the inevitable published accounts that followed these visits. Although statements about trading activities are plentiful, they are seldom detailed; thus it is not possible to reconstruct the actual mechanics of the fur trade to the degree of completeness that is desirable.

In neighboring areas of southwestern Alaska, however, the Alaska Commercial Company and other American firms were not so generous with credit as their predecessors had been. In the Lake Iliamna area, for example, credit to the Tanaina Indians was halted and an attempt was made to reduce the indebtedness of the people (Porter, 1893, pp. 247-51; Townsend, n.d.). On Kodiak Island the Alaska Commercial Company and other traders, after having followed a credit policy similar to that of the Russian-American Company, suddenly shifted to an exchange business and attempted to collect debts. This worked a great hardship on the Eskimos (DRHA, vol. 2, pp. 186-87). In Prince William Sound the Alaska Commercial Company extended unlimited credit and paid high prices for furs while it was necessary to compete with rival companies, but then halted credit, lowered

fur prices, and attempted to collect debts as soon as competition
had been eliminated. The Eskimos thus found themselves
charged with debts which they could not possibly pay for years.
When a trapper brought in furs, half their value was applied to
his outstanding debt and the rest he exchanged for trade goods.
As a result of this arrangement, many Eskimos became discour-
aged and trapped only when compelled to by pressing needs
(Abercrombie, 1900, p. 400). Since the Alaska Commercial Company never had any serious competition in the Nushagak River
region, it is likely that they quickly abandoned the paternalistic
credit system of the Russian-American Company and refused to
allow the Eskimos to run up large debts. Whether or not the
Company attempted to collect outstanding debts is not known.
Whatever the effect of this policy shift on the Eskimos, the Alaska
Commercial Company post at Nushagak maintained a moderately flourishing trade with the people of the area at least through
the remainder of the nineteenth century.

Charles Bryant, when he visited the Nushagak post in the summer of 1868, noted that beaver was the principal fur and that
more than 2,000 skins were taken in by the post annually. Bryant
talked to the "chief" at Nushagak and asked whether the number
could be increased. The "chief" complained about restrictions on
the sale of ammunition and the small amount that was allowed to
the Nushagak post; "he said with a grim smile, 'more powder,
more fur.'" Apparently only 300 pounds of powder had been al-
lotted to the post during the previous year and Bryant believed
that 2,500 people depended on this allowance, an average of less
than a pound for eight persons per year. The Russians had placed
no restrictions on the sale of ammunition and those in effect at
the time of Bryant's visit may have been fixed by the Company as
a precautionary measure (Bryant and McIntyre, 1869, p. 23).

During the 1870's, beaver, muskrat, land otter, and red fox
seem to have been the most important fur bearing animals in the
Nushagak region and Elliott, writing in 1875, said that the mink
and muskrat in the area were not of so fine a quality as those
taken in the Kuskokwim region. The beaver and land otter pelts
were of particularly fine quality and all other animals were taken
in relatively small quantities. There was also a small trade in
swansdown and caribou skins were dried and traded (Elliott,

1875, p. 40). The only information on the relative value of furs during this period comes from a short list of fur costs included by Father Shishkin in his journal for 1878 (DRHA, vol. 1, p. 329):

beaver	$ .10 to	$1.20
sable	.10 to	1.20
fox	.20 to	.80
sea otter and mink	.10 to	.50
bluish-gray fox	1.00 to	1.50
deerskins	.20 to	.50

Presumably these dollar evaluations refer to the value of the trade goods that were exchanged for furs.

The trade in swansdown, although not mentioned by Shishkin, seems to have increased during the following decade. Trumpeter swans were taken at night when the Eskimos noiselessly paddled up to them as they slept. Muskrats too seem to have been killed in increasing numbers even though their value remained low. The traders were forced to accept muskrat pelts in order to secure other more valuable furs (Elliott, 1886, p. 399).

At this period, in the 1880's and 1890's, a clearer picture of the organization of the Alaska Commercial Company emerges. The company apparently had four main stations: Unalaska, St. Michael, Kodiak, and the Pribilof Islands. Nushagak, one of the Company's less important posts, was in the Kuskokwim Division and was administered from Unalaska. About the year 1880 John W. Clark became principal trader at Nushagak and remained until his death in 1897. During this time his trade in furs reputedly amounted to around $10,000 annually, a figure presumably based on prices paid for the furs by a wholesaler in the states. At various times between 1880 and 1890 the Nushagak post maintained outstations at Ugashik and Togiak. It is also possible that there were additional minor stations at various points on the Nushagak River, placed in such a manner as to control the trapping activity of the Nushagak River Eskimos (Kitchener, 1954, p. 164; Report of the Governor of Alaska. . . . 1891, pub. 1891, p. 25; Jackson, 1886, p. 55; Malach, 1950, p. 7).

The enumerator of the Eleventh Census also speaks of a number of subsidiary outposts throughout the Nushagak River region, each one under the direction of a native trader who, at certain seasons of the year, brought the furs he had purchased to Nushagak. As many as 4,000 pelts a year were obtained in this manner, not including ground squirrel and muskrat skins. Among these, surprisingly enough, were sea otter skins obtained by Bristol Bay Eskimos who were encouraged by John Clark to hunt them in the Cook Inlet region (Porter, 1893, pp. 95-96, 253).

One outstation of the Nushagak post appears to have been located at the mouth of the Mulchatna River. This small station, in existence in 1896 and probably somewhat earlier, was called Middle Station. In the winter of 1896, a man named Jackson, an assistant to John Clark at Nushagak, accompanied the Moravian missionaries on a trip up the river to collect pelts at Middle Station and also inventory the trade goods on hand there (Baker, 1902, p. 284; Alaska Records, 1892-1938, p. 54). (During the summer of 1964, the author was unable to locate the site of this small trading station.)

An item of trade that appears to have been important during the early American period, but that had almost disappeared by the end of the nineteenth century, was walrus ivory. Walrus were hunted on the shoals off Hagemeister Island and along the north coast of the Alaska Peninsula. The Eskimos of Bristol Bay were known for their skill as ivory carvers (Porter, 1893, p. 253; Swineford, 1898, pp. 162-163).

After John Clark's death in 1897, his trader at Ugashik, a man named Mittendorf, came to Nushagak to take over the post. Later Carl Hall ran the store for Mittendorf but by this time Nushagak was experiencing its decline. When Hall died in 1934, the long history of trading in the village came to an end.

Not until after the turn of the century is there ample information about trading activity in the Nushagak River region other than that controlled by the Alaska Commercial Company. During the summer of 1902 the biological survey party under the direction of Wilfred H. Osgood and proceeding from Iliamna Lake to Nushagak obtained much needed provisions at the mouth of the Mulchatna River at "the cabin where remnants of the supplies of the defunct Trans-Alaska Company were for sale" (Ogsood, 1904, p. 14). This company was conducting surveys for a proposed railroad line which was to run from Iliamna Bay to Anvik. Osgood's statement would seem to suggest that a representative of this company was disposing of equipment and supplies to residents of the area. As early as 1900 an elderly trader named Ivan McKinley lived at Kokwok. He was baptized by the Moravians in April of that year (Alaska Material, box vi, Records of Ecclesiastical Acts, no. 3, 1888-1902). A man named William Hurley lived at Ekwok from before the turn of the century until his death in the early 1930's. He was a prospector and part-time trader. An informant at Ekwok in 1964 remembered that a trapper had had a small cabin at the mouth of the Mulchatna about 1927 and had done a little trading during the summer months. In the 1930's three different men, including Hurley, maintained trading posts at the now abandoned village of Nunachuak (Mertie, 1938, p. 25).

Evidently, then, there has been some kind of trading activity by independent traders along the river almost continuously since the turn of the century with at least one trader being more or less permanently established. These were probably one-man operations and involved individuals who combined trapping and prospecting with a little trading. At the present time there are no stores in any of the three Nushagak River villages. Informants reported that in recent years someone from Dillingham had started a small store at New Stuyahok but had quickly run up a debt of more than $9,000 and had been forced to close. The necessity of allowing large amounts of credit means that anyone starting a store must have a sizable amount of capital back of the venture. Most of the Eskimos purchase heavily in Dillingham at the end of the fishing season and frequently receive an advance from the canneries for doing this.

During the first three decades of the twentieth century the Wood and Nushagak River drainages remained highly productive trapping areas, particularly for beaver, although trapping activity had declined after the beginning of the salmon canning industry in the mid 1880's. In 1924 furs valued at more than a quarter of a million dollars were taken out of the entire southwestern Alaska region (Report of the Governor of Alaska. . . . 1925, pub. 1925, p. 76), and in the early 1930's beaver and fox are spoken of as being plentiful in the Mulchatna area and constituting the main source of commercial fur (Mertie, 1938, p. 35). More recently, however, owing to overtrapping and perhaps some natural causes, the beaver population has dropped drastically. As a result, in 1951 the Fish and Wildlife Service closed the entire Wood and Nushagak river drainages to beaver trapping, and mink then became the most sought after fur bearer. In the spring of 1958 the entire watershed was reopened to trapping with a limit of fifteen beaver to each trapper (Rogers, 1955, p. 11; Hawkins and Daugherty, 1958, pp. 32-33).

We have seen the Nushagak post emerge as an important trading center for the entire region of southwestern Alaska immediately after the first Russian penetration of the area, only to decline as other settlements and better lines of communication were established. In the American period the post maintained its importance as the central base in the Nushagak region for the trading of furs and obtaining of supplies, and so powerful was the Alaska Commercial Company that independent traders or rival companies never gained a foothold in the area. The growth of the commercial fishing industry in Bristol Bay also aided the Nushagak post and its outlying stations at Togiak and Ugashik since a certain amount of trade with the canneries and cannery employes was always conducted. Toward the close of the nineteenth century, however, the fur trade and traders as agents of change were overshadowed by the next historical development to be discussed: the phenomenal growth of the commercial fishing industry.

IV

The Commercial Fishing Industry

◆◆

● OF ALL THE AGENTS OF CHANGE DISCUSSED IN THIS STUDY, NONE HAD
a greater or more lasting effect on the Eskimos of the Nushagak
River region than the commercial fishing industry that began to
develop in Bristol Bay during the 1890's. This remarkable industry, one of the most significant commercial innovations in Alaska's
history, has, from its inception, brought about significant and far-
reaching changes in the area. In the early days commercial fishing
caused major seasonal fluctuations in population which brought
the Eskimos into first-hand contact with many different races and
nationalities. Even today, when a sizable American town has
grown up at the mouth of the Nushagak River and the economy
is more diversified than at any time in the past, the fishing season
is still of the greatest importance and is the one activity in which
everyone takes part, whether or not he has other sources of income.

There are five species of Pacific salmon: the king or chinook,
the red or sockeye, the pink or humpback, the chum or dog, and
the silver or coho. All these salmon make spawning runs into the
rivers of Bristol Bay, but the red salmon is by far the most important species from a commercial standpoint. The rivers flowing
into Bristol Bay are the greatest red salmon spawning grounds in
the world. This is because the red salmon spawns only in lakes, or
in streams that flow into or out of lakes. Most of the rivers
flowing into Bristol Bay have numerous lakes at their headwaters.
It is no exaggeration to say that red salmon are the life blood of

Bristol Bay (Hawkins and Daugherty, 1958, p. 16). Vast numbers of fish have been canned in past years and packs of a million or more cans have not been unusual.

The fishing season begins in June but few salmon are caught until the big runs commence in July. "Then the tempo of fishing and processing builds up to a hectic pace for a few short days, after which the peak runs have passed up the rivers and the fishing season is virtually over. Many fishermen earn ninety per cent of their yearly income in two weeks" (Hawkins and Daugherty, 1958, p. 16).

Both gill nets and fish traps were used in the early days of the commercial fishery to obtain fish for canning. The gill net proved to be a useful device because the water is murky at the mouth of the Nushagak, and the fish cannot see the nets. The swift tides and muddy bottom of the bay region, however, are unsuitable for traps and they were never extensively used even before 1923 when regulations forbidding their use went into effect.

The production of the Bristol Bay fishery has varied greatly over the years but the general trend of the pack, at least since 1938, has been downward. The reasons for this decline are not clearly understood and have been the subject of much debate, some of it acrimonious, among fishermen, cannery operators, representatives of the United States Fish and Wildlife Service, and, since 1959, employes of the Alaska Department of Fish and Game. The years of unregulated fishing have doubtless taken their toll, but scientists also feel that biological factors may be partly responsible for the decline. At any rate, the decline in the number of fish has forced changes in the methods of operation and also in the type of gear that is used.

The early gill net boats were twenty-five foot Columbia River double enders with a center board and spirit sail. These boats were operated by two men, one of whom handled the net and the other the boat. Gradually the design of the boats improved and in 1922 the first power boats were brought into bay and purse seiners were introduced the same year. Seiners and power boats proved to be extremely efficient at catching fish and the federal regulating authorities felt they would endanger the run were they allowed to continue. In addition, the cannery operators realized that their tight control over the fishery would be weakened if seiners and power boats, worked by independent operators, were allowed to come into Bristol Bay. As a result, regulations were passed outlawing these kinds of equipment.

The sailboat, being less maneuverable and much slower than the power boat, was naturally less efficient in finding and catching fish. Eventually the canneries, eager to process more fish, began to look for ways to circumvent the restriction on power boats. This they were able to accomplish by means of a towboat that could tie on a number of sailboats and tow them to the fishing grounds. In this way the sailboats could be moved rapidly when necessary and they soon became almost as efficient as the power boats. As a result, the Fish and Wildlife Service removed the restriction on the power units in 1951, and these boats, up to a length of thirty-two feet, are permitted to operate in Bristol Bay.

With the advent of power, a major economic revolution occurred in the bay. Prior to 1951 private ownership of fishing boats and gear was almost unknown. The canneries owned the boats and gear and hired fishermen to man them, usually bringing most of the workers from the States. Power boats were an efficient fishing outfit that some local fishermen could afford and since independent operators received far more for their fish than did the men working for the canneries, the number of privately owned boats rapidly increased. The trend also strengthened the bargaining power of local fishermen who, since they were independent of the canneries, were able to get a better price for their fish.

As previously mentioned, the only device used to catch salmon commercially in Bristol Bay is the gill net. This is a strong net of linen or nylon with meshes that vary in size according to the species of salmon being sought. The salmon swim part way through and are caught, usually just behind the gills. They then must be removed by hand when the net is "picked." The nets are suspended in the water by using wooden or plastic floats along one edge and lead sinkers along the other. In Bristol Bay most nets are used as free floating or "drift" nets, but some are anchored and these "set" nets are placed along the beach in locations where the fisherman thinks he will have good luck. These set net locations are registered and a fisherman usually retains the same one for a number of years. The net extends at right angles from the beach, and is anchored to stakes that have been driven in place when the tide is out.

The drift net is operated from a boat in deep water anywhere within the fishing district. The net may be 150 fathoms (900 feet) long and only one net can be operated from a boat. At the beginning of a fishing period, the fisherman runs out his net and the boat and net then drift with the tide. He can pick up his gear at any time during the fishing period, which is usually twenty-four hours but may last much longer after the peak runs have passed, and deliver his fish to the cannery or to a cannery scow that comes out to collect the fish so that the fishermen will not have to leave the grounds.

In Bristol Bay fishing is not permitted in the main body of the bay, but is restricted to the mouths of the major streams entering the bay. Early investigations by the Fish and Wildlife Service determined that the main body of the bay was a great schooling ground where fish from all the rivers mingled before separating to make their spawning runs up the rivers. By restricting fishing to the river mouths, the activity can be controlled more effectively. In the early days of the industry, fishermen commonly fished right in the rivers. In fact, in 1890 the four canneries in Nushagak Bay worked together to build a salmon trap that stretched across the Wood River leaving only a gap of 100 feet in the middle. This was called to the attention of Lieutenant Commander Z. L. Tanner, commanding the U.S. Fish Commission Streamer *Albatross*, who reported the trap as a violation of law because it was felt that the Eskimos living along the river would lose their main means of livelihood (McDonald, 1894, p. 6). Probably as a result of a number of acts similar to this one, and because of fears that under these circumstances few salmon were escaping up the rivers to spawn when the fishermen were allowed to operate in the rivers, both the Wood and Nushagak rivers, and for that matter all other rivers flowing into Bristol Bay, were closed to commercial fishing after the season of 1907 and have remained closed to the present time (Marsh and Cobb, 1911a, p. 34).

The established fishing districts are named for the various rivers entering Bristol Bay. From south to north in a counterclockwise direction around the bay, they are: the Ugashik, Egegik, Naknek-Kvichak, Nushagak, and Togiak (see map 2). These districts are marked with upper and lower limits beyond which fishing is not permitted. Each district is individually regulated according to the abundance of fish and this factor determines the length of the fishing periods. A boat is not permitted to shift from one district to another without giving notice to the Alaska Department of Fish and Game and waiting for a period of twenty-four hours (most of the above material, except where indicated, has been taken from Hawkins and Daugherty, 1958).

It is now necessary to turn our attention to the history of commercial fishing with specific reference to the locations of particular canneries and the rise and decline in their numbers from the earliest period until the present. Here we will be dealing specifically with Nushagak Bay and no attempt will be made, except in a general way, to trace such development for the rest of the Bristol Bay region.

Although the Russian-American Company intended to establish a commercial fishery at Alexandrovski in 1866 (Russian-American Company Records: Communications Sent, vol. 47, no. 127, folio 42), the earliest commercial fishing in the Nushagak River region was carried out by the Alaska Commercial Company at Nushagak for salting purposes. Petroff mentions that the company exported from 800 to 1,200 barrels of salted salmon each year but it is not certain when this activity began (Petroff, 1884, p. 16). In 1883 the schooner *Neptune* visited Nushagak Bay on a salting trip that was, in reality, a prospecting venture since the preceding year successful canneries had been established on Kodiak Island and along Cook Inlet. In the summer of 1883 cannery buildings were erected by the Arctic Packing Company which began operations the following year with a pack of 400 cases. The invention of the canning process provided a means by which the Alaska salmon runs could be utilized much more fully. It was no longer necessary to salt the fish for preservation (Hawkins and Daugherty, 1958, p. 17; Moser, 1899, pp. 16-17, 173-174; Cobb, 1931, pp. 462-463).

The plant of the Arctic Packing Company was not only the first cannery in Nushagak Bay, but the first to operate along the Bering Sea. It was located close to the Eskimo village of Kanulik near the site where the Moravian mission of Carmel was established two years later. It is sometimes known as Ralph's cannery and at the height of its activity at the end of the nineteenth century had a capacity of 2,000 cases a day. In 1885 the Alaska Packing Company erected a cannery on the west side of the bay about a mile and one-half below the junction of the Wood and Nushagak rivers. This has been popularly known in the region as the Scandinavian cannery and was in operation almost continually until just after the Second World War. The following year the Bristol Bay Canning Company, a San Francisco firm, built a cannery on the western shore of Nushagak Bay at the mouth of a small creek about two miles below the Scandinavian cannery. At a later date, this place was referred to as Dillingham and then Kanakanak but when the cannery was built it was popularly known as the Bradford cannery. The Eskimo village of Kanakanak was located less than a mile below the Bradford cannery which was operated each year until 1907 and was dismantled shortly thereafter (Cobb, 1931, pp. 462-463; Moser, 1899, pp. 173-174; Rogers, 1955, p. 4) (see map 3).

In 1888 economic development of Nushagak Bay shifted back to the east bank with the erection, by the Nushagak Canning Company, of a fourth cannery at a place called Stugarok, or Clark's Point, about six miles below Nushagak. (John W. Clark of Nushagak may have operated a salting station at this point prior to the erection of the cannery [Malach, 1950, p. 7].) Between 1892 and 1901 this cannery was not operated, but in 1901 a larger cannery was built and began operations. It produced a salmon pack for many years, but recently has been held in reserve and used as a fishing station (Rogers, 1955, p. 4; Cobb, 1931, pp. 462-463; Moser, 1899, pp. 173-174; Moser, 1902, p. 202).

The years 1888 and 1889 saw a marked increase in the number of canneries operating throughout southwestern and southeastern Alaska, and their large output called the public's attention to the Alaska salmon fishery for the first time. However, there was over-expansion in these years which resulted in serious price declines and near bankruptcy for some companies. Therefore a movement was started to unify control over the production and marketing of canned salmon. In the beginning this move consisted simply of cooperative working agreements between several independent cannery owners. Marketing pools were formed and quotas assigned to individual plants. Some canneries were closed in order

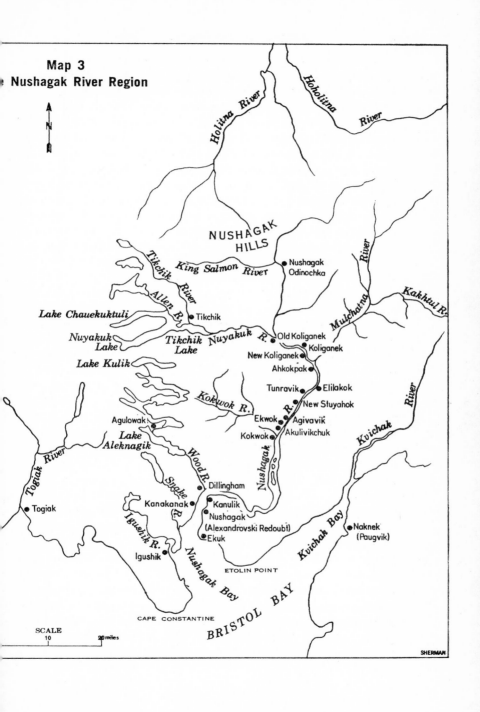

Map 3
Nushagak River Region

N

NUSHAGAK
HILLS

Holitna River

Hoholitna River

King Salmon River

Nushagak
Odinochka

Tikchik River

Allen R.

Lake Chauekuktuli

Tikchik

Nuyakuk Lake

Tikchik Lake

Nuyakuk R.

Old Koliganek

Mulchatna

Kakhtul R.

Lake Kulik

New Koliganek

Koliganek

Ahkokpak

Tunravik

Elilakok

Kokwok R.

New Stuyahok

R.

Kvichak River

Agulowak

Ekwok

Agivavik

Lake Aleknagik

Kokwok

Akulivikchuk

Wood R.

Nushagak

Kvichak

Togiak River

Snake R.

Dillingham

Kvichak Bay

Togiak

Kanakanak

Kanulik

Nushagak
(Alexandrovski Redoubt)

Naknek
(Paugvik)

Igushik R.

Ekuk

Igushik

ETOLIN POINT

Nushagak Bay

CAPE CONSTANTINE

BRISTOL BAY

SCALE
10   20 miles

SHERMAN

to restrict the output that was forcing down prices. An outgrowth of this early movement to control the output of the salmon canneries was the Alaska Packing Association which was formed in 1892. Essentially a profit sharing organization, it included thirty-one canneries of which nine continued to operate while the others were closed. In 1893 the organization was incorporated as the Alaska Packers Association and the members exchanged plants for capital stock (Gregory and Barnes, 1939, pp. 93-94). The Association always centered its activity in the Bristol Bay region and all the early Nushagak Bay canneries previously mentioned joined in its first year. In 1897 these three operating canneries employed 144 white fishermen, 38 white, 306 Chinese, and 40 native cannery workers (Moser, 1899, p. 174). In 1900, the same canneries employed 215 white fishermen, 66 white, 450 Chinese, and 75 native cannery hands (Moser, 1902, p. 202).

Toward the close of the nineteenth century, particularly after 1897, individuals independent of the canneries in Nushagak Bay commonly established salting stations in order to legally reserve a potential cannery site that might be of value at a future date. These saltery owners would use their own boats and either sell fresh fish to the canneries or ship salted salmon in barrels to the States. One salting station, that of C. E. Whitney & Company, was built and operated by the Bristol Bay Canning Company on The Snake River in 1886. In 1889 it was moved to the mouth of the Nushagak River and about 1892 to the east side of the bay one and one-half miles above Kanulik. In 1900 this saltery employed 62 white fishermen, trapmen and saltery hands, and 3 Eskimos (Porter, 1893, p. 95; Cobb, 1931, pp. 462-463; Moser, 1899, pp. 173-174; 1902, p. 205).

In 1899 the Pacific Steam Whaling Company erected a cannery on the eastern shore of Nushagak Bay at Nushagak and the same year the Alaska Fishermen's Packing Company built one just below it. The Pacific Packing and Navigation Company purchased the former in 1901 and upon the sale of its properties in 1904 became a part of the Northwestern Fisheries Company. Control of the second Nushagak cannery passed to Libby, McNeil, and Libby in 1913. Both are said to have been abandoned in the 1930's (Cobb, 1931, pp. 462-463).

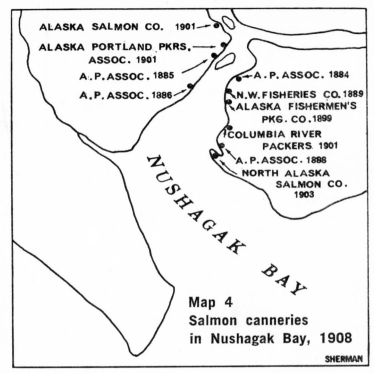

ALASKA SALMON CO. 1901

ALASKA PORTLAND PKRS.
ASSOC. 1901

A. P. ASSOC. 1885

A. P. ASSOC. 1886

A. P. ASSOC. 1884

N.W. FISHERIES CO. 1889
ALASKA FISHERMEN'S
PKG. CO. 1899

COLUMBIA RIVER
PACKERS 1901

A. P. ASSOC. 1888

NORTH ALASKA
SALMON CO.
1903

NUSHAGAK BAY

Map 4
Salmon canneries
in Nushagak Bay, 1908

SHERMAN

In 1901 the Columbia River Packers Association, the Alaska-Portland Packers Association, and the Alaska Salmon Company built canneries on Nushagak Bay. The Alaska Salmon Company operated the Wood River cannery at the mouth of that river. All these canneries were operated more or less continuously, at least until the early 1930's, and one is still in operation under different ownership. In 1903 the North Alaska Salmon Company opened a cannery at Ekuk less than a mile below Clark's Point. This cannery was later sold to Libby, McNeil, and Libby and is still in operation today (Cobb, 1931, pp. 462-463).

The accompanying map (4) based on Freeman (1908) shows the arrangement of salmon canneries in Nushagak Bay at about this time. Ten canneries were in operation and the heaviest concentration of population was on the east side of the bay. The number of canneries shown on the map seems to have been about the maximum number to operate in Nushagak Bay although a few more may have sprung up, particularly near the mouth of the Igushik River. In Bristol Bay as a whole, the number of canneries gradually increased until in 1920 when twenty-five were in operation. Floating canneries first appeared in 1922 and freezer ships have operated in the area since the Second World War. In the 1930's there were, from time to time, sharp curtailments of fishing for conservation purposes. Also improvements in cannery machinery made it advisable for the canneries to consolidate their units into a smaller number of larger units. During this period major efforts were made to deal with the declining numbers of salmon. Six canneries closed in the Nushagak Bay region in 1935, and only one shore cannery and two floating canneries operated that year. The following year the number rose to eight but in 1938 only two functioned owing to lengthy labor disputes at the beginning of the season; in 1939 six canneries were in operation. These figures are mentioned to show the amount of fluctuation during the period after about 1910 and to suggest that the Nushagak Bay salmon canning business, at least in terms of numbers of canneries operating, never again flourished as it did during the first decade of this century (Bower, 1938, pp. 26-29; Hawkins and Daugherty, 1958, p. 17). After 1940 there was a general decline in the number of fish caught as shown in the accompanying table, which, at the time of writing, is the most up-to-date chart available to show the catch in the Nushagak fishing district.

1940	166,208	1950	115,019
1941	172,835	1951	31,143
1942	196,671	1952	81,720
1943	282,100	1953	36,544
1944	270,034	1954	51,446
1945	222,738	1955	85,573
1946	151,216	1956	106,943
1947	220,181	1957	78,587
1948	262,581	1958	176,690
1949	79,173	1959	182,466

(Anonymous, 1960, p. 61)

There were peak fishing years in 1943, 1944, 1947, 1948, and again in 1958 and 1959, but a steady decrease in the pack will be noted, particularly since 1948. The Nushagak fishing district has not only suffered the downward trend noted above, but has also dropped as a percentage of the total Bristol Bay catch (Rogers, 1955, p. 4). The reasons for this steady decline are doubtless multiple and beyond the scope of this study.[1]

As important as the commercial salmon fishery has been in the economic history of Alaska and as intrinsically interesting as is the development of this industry in Nushagak Bay, we would not be concerned with it here were it not for the profound effect of the history and development of commercial fishing on the Eskimos of the region. Therefore, our major focus will be on tracing the development of Eskimo involvement in the industry with particular emphasis on the pattern of employment through the years.

As early as 1887 the Moravian missionaries noted how large numbers of Eskimos were attracted to Carmel and other points on the bay during the fishing season (Report of the Commissioner of Education. . . . 1887-1888, pub. 1889, p. 186), and we know that tent settlements sprang up near the canneries every summer (Norton, 1911, p. 27). From the beginning most of the actual fishing was by Euro-Americans who came to Alaska for the fishing season and returned to the States when the runs were over and the canneries had completed their packs. Most of the work in the canneries was done by Chinese laborers with supervisory jobs falling to Euro-Americans. The first cannery methods were slow and clumsy, the hand labor often producing an inferior product (Gregory and Barnes, 1939, p. 27).

From the beginning, operators of the salmon canning industry in Nushagak Bay seem to have made little or no effort to utilize the local labor supply. Bishop Bachman, on a tour of inspection of the Moravian missions in Alaska during the summer of 1891, noted that an occasional Eskimo was employed by the canneries but that in general the Chinese were considered much more reliable and methodical (SPG Proceedings, 1891, p. 75). A somewhat more favorable situation, from the standpoint of the Eskimos, is suggested by the statistics of the Alaska Salmon pack for the 1894

[1] For a detailed study of the various factors affecting the decline of the Alaska salmon canning industry the reader is referred to Richard A. Cooley's excellent study, "Politics and Conservation, the Decline of the Alaska Salmon," 1963.

season which show that at three canneries listed as being located at "Nushagak," out of a total of 468 employed persons, 128 were "natives" (Report of the Governor of Alaska. . . . 1895, pub. 1895, p. 12). Porter notes that at about this same time "native" cannery workers in the Nushagak district were averaging $48.50 per month during an average period of operation of sixty-three days (Porter, 1893, p. 218). At this time more Eskimos were employed in the small salteries than in the canneries and those working at the salting stations apparently earned less than cannery workers. We have already noted that in 1897 only 40 "natives" were employed by the member canneries of the Alaska Packers Association and these were paid at an average of from $1.00 to $1.50 per day (Moser, 1899, p. 177).

As early as 1898 government officials deplored the fact that a greater number of local residents were not employed in the fishery throughout southwestern and southeastern Alaska. In that year, J. G. Brady, governor of Alaska, noted in his annual report to the Secretary of the Interior that "It is to be regretted that the natives of western Alaska cannot be employed more and taught to do the work which is now entrusted to the imported Chinese" (Report of the Governor of Alaska. . . . 1898, pub. 1898, p. 34). The following year, in response to complaints about the failure of the canneries to use local labor, the governor commented:

> When the fish are caught, they must be canned without delay, and to do this men who are trained and used to it are necessary. They [the canneries] cannot then undertake to deal with natives and others who have no training whatever, and who have no compunction in breaking a contract and leaving their work in the middle of the season (Report of the Governor of Alaska. . . . 1899, pub. 1899, p. 7).

A federal employe, writing at about the same time and specifically about the Nushagak River region, also regrets that the natives cannot be depended upon. His statement is relatively detailed and seems to reflect accurately local attitudes toward the employment of Eskimos.

> The canneries gladly employ every native who is willing to work; nay, more, they seek for this labor in the villages and offer every inducement for them to work, and would employ many more if they could be obtained and were reliable. This is not done for

charity's sake—the canneries are not in the field for that purpose, though they are far from being uncharitable—but because the labor is needed, particularly when the rush is on, and for which profitable provision cannot otherwise be made.

When the cannery ships arrive in the spring the native, having struggled through a long, severe winter, is hungry and has many wants. He greets the cannery ships with childish glee and wishes work. It is given him, his hunger is appeased from the overflowing cannery table, his daily wages soon supply the few luxuries he desires, and then he no longer cares for work. Why should he work? Hunger no longer worries him, his immediate wants are satisfied, and he has no others!

The condition of native labor is the same here, among the Eskimo, as it is in other sections of Alaska, . . . ; only here the canneryman, being entirely out of the lines of communication with the labor market, seems still more desirous of employing natives and frequently sends some distance to their villages to enlist them in his work. Statistics show that the largest number employed in any one cannery is from 25 to 30 for a short period. Some days there may be 40 and the next only 10.

It is true that the canneries can not give them constant employment as their intelligence only warrants giving them certain work; still a good, reliable native will have work the greater part of the time, and can earn during the short season from $100 to $125, also having his board furnished him during the time employed.

The wages paid this year to adult males was $2 per day; reliable men received $2.25; boys from 12 to 14 years of age received $1 per day and children were seen piling cans who were not more than 6 years of age, and who received 50 cents a day. They demand and receive their wages daily.

Formerly the wage of adult males was $1.50 per day, but in the early part of this season a 'walking delegate,' in the shape of a 'tyone' (chief), appeared at the canneries and the natives struck for $2 and promptly got it.

Money seems to have no value to the native except to satisfy his immediate wants, and the traders cater to their taste for gewgaws by supplying them with things for which they have no use. They have a fancy for cuckoo clocks and watches, though they cannot read the time; cheap jewelry and perfume; and a silk dress is more than tempting. One woman was noticed wearing the usual skin trousers and boots, and over all a velvetine dress, well tucked up, and as greasy as if it had been soaked in a pot of rancid oil. As before mentioned, the canneries supply board to all the natives employed; the food is abundant to the point of wastefulness; it is of excellent quality, well cooked, in large variety, and given with a generous hand; none need go hungry; even the hun-

dreds of sled dogs from the villages greet the cannery ships, gather
around the canneries during the season, and grow fat, sleek, lazy,
and good natured.

Of the large supplies of food carried up in the spring a considerable quantity usually remains over when the cannery closes.
This is stored at some of the canneries and the watchman is instructed to distribute food in case of distress.

There can be no doubt that the canneries have benefited the
native by adding to his physical comfort. The fish supply for his
use has not been reduced; . . . if he is willing to work he can earn
money and procure civilized comforts. Whether his contact with
the fishermen and Chinese during their yearly visits adds anything
to his moral well-being is a question, but he suffers no more here
than natives do in all parts of the world when they come in contact with our civilization (Moser, 1902, pp. 185-187).

This quotation suggests that some Eskimos were able to obtain
employment in the canneries even during the earliest years of the
industry in spite of considerable prejudice against them and their
abilities as workers. In this connection is worth noting that in
1900 the two canneries at Nushagak employed 70 local people as
opposed to 193 Chinese (Moser, 1902, pp. 203-204). Even when
Chinese contract labor was readily available, the canneries in
Nushagak Bay could not maintain production without hiring
some Eskimos, particularly at the peak of the salmon runs.

The Moravian missionaries at Carmel, predictably, were more
concerned than a government employe like Moser about the
moral effect of the "heathen" cannery workers on the Eskimos.
They particularly deplored the fact that the Chinese introduced
intoxicating beverages and taught the Eskimos how to make
them. In 1900 a missionary noted that

The great curse of the natives is still drink. It is considered amusing
to drink until they lie around like dogs. The whites as well as the
Chinese bring whiskey into the country. The people earn so much
at the canneries that they do not know what to do with their
money. Then the Chinaman comes and coaxes them to buy all kinds
of trash. The canneries paid from 75¢ a day for a little boy to $3
a day for a man. I have known one man to sell $25 worth of King
salmon in one day (SPG Proceedings, 1900, pp. 54-55).

Eskimos were attracted to the canneries even when not employed there. In 1905 the Moravian Bishop Hamilton observed
disapprovingly that many Eskimos found it easier to utilize the

waste of the canneries than to make their own fish traps and secure their winter's supply of fish by "patient work." The bishop
also commented on the evils of drink and his statements have the
ring of defeat as he doubtless contemplated the imminent closing
of the mission at Carmel.

> Nor is it a wonder that they catch the spirit of the immoral, the
> drink-loving and the gamblers and imbibe from the Asiatic heathen
> new vices. It is not strange that when the few missionaries set up
> Christian standards, the ignorant Eskimos regard them as very
> exceptional men, who are making demands such as the average
> man considers quite needless. To complete the dark picture it must
> be added, that the Chinese in particular have taught the natives to
> brew and distill a terrible kind of drink. Graham flour, brown sugar
> and water are mixed so as to form a horrid mash, which is first
> allowed to ferment and then distilled. I was informed that very
> few men on the Nushagak can resist the temptation to concoct
> this fearful drink. Cases of church discipline are frequently con-
> nected with it, or with a disregard for the law of sexual purity
> (Hamilton, 1906, p. 33).

The salmon canning procedure, which used hand labor almost
exclusively during the early years of the industry, soon began to
introduce improvements in the process of transforming fish into a
canned product. The most significant of these improvements was
a remarkable machine called the "Iron Chink," first used in 1903,
which beheaded, split, and cleaned the fish. Its name, of course,
derives from the fact that it replaced Chinese labor. The "Iron
Chink" was introduced on a large scale between 1911 and 1913
and the introduction of high speed cannery lines took place in the
1920's. This mechanization reduced the necessary labor by about
three quarters, a factor that should be kept in mind with regard
to employment practices in the Nushagak River region (Gregory
and Barnes, 1939, p. 27).

In 1912 over seventy per cent of the fishermen in southeastern
Alaska were Indians while in the southwestern area very few Eskimos were employed. It is not clear whether this figure refers to
both fishermen and cannery workers, but presumably it does
(Anonymous, 1913, p. 51). Both government and trade publications of this period frequently carry statements defending this situation. The trade journals in particular often point out that the
type of work performed in western Alaska canneries by Chinese

could not be successfully accomplished by natives (Anonymous, 1913, p. 51; Pacific Fisherman, 1912, p. 16). Government publications profess to be gratified by the gradual increase in the number of natives engaged in the fisheries and usually look forward to the time when all the labor in the fishing industry will be obtained locally (Report of the Governor of Alaska. . . . 1916, pub. 1916, p. 17).

Doubtless, in southeastern Alaska the employers were in closer touch with the labor market and could deal quickly with any defections in their fishing and canning gangs. Whether true or not, employers in western Alaska felt that the Eskimos in their region could not be depended upon and they continued to rely heavily on imported labor. The Chinese laborer, bound to a contract that virtually enslaved him to his employer, and transported far from home, could do nothing to protest his working conditions even if he were inclined to do so. The canneries could never hope to obtain such a hold over local labor.

Cannery operators in the Nushagak River region very likely began to experience difficulty in obtaining Chinese laborers after the indefinite extension of the Chinese Exclusion Act in 1904. By 1918 Filipino and Mexican workers outnumbered the Chinese and there seems also to have been an increasingly large number of Eskimos employed. One aspect of the industry, however, in which the Eskimos were extremely slow to participate was the actual fishing. From the earliest time, as we have noted, the fishing was done by men brought from the States (Roberts, 1940, p. 4). As late as 1929 there were only twenty-eight resident boats in all of Bristol Bay and these were owned by whites or mixed-bloods. Nor did the canneries buy fish from the Eskimo set-netters; there was a feeling that their fish would be dirty and poorly handled. Shortly after 1929 a few Eskimos began using sailboats and gear supplied by the canneries. In other words, they became "cannery fishermen" and were obliged to sell their fish to the cannery that provided their equipment.

The distinction between "cannery" and "independent" fishermen merits brief attention at this point. The cannery fisherman fishes with a company-owned boat and all his line, nets, and other equipment are furnished by the cannery. He can live in the company bunkhouse when he is not fishing, and his meals are also furnished. The independent fisherman, on the other hand, possesses, or is in the process of buying, his own boat and fishing equipment. He usually sleeps and eats on his boat and is responsible for all his expenses. The independent fisherman may finance the purchase of his boat through a cannery and contract to sell all his catch to that cannery until the payments are completed. After that, he is free to make any arrangements that he chooses. Today most cannery fishermen come from outside the Bristol Bay area whereas most of the independent fishermen are residents of the general region.

In 1937 the resident fishermen in Bristol Bay formed the Bering Sea Fishermen's Union as a local of the Alaska Fishermen's Union, a much older organization founded in 1902. Resident cannery workers also became members of this local, the major goal of which was to achieve precedence for residents not only in the canneries but as fishermen. Although not primarily concerned with Eskimo employment as a separate problem from the employment of Bristol Bay and Alaskan residents in general, the factors that led to the establishment of a local union branch supporting local interests are reflected in the fact that in 1937 only 194 Eskimos were employed as cannery workers in southwestern Alaska out of a total of 4,328. Orientals and Latin Americans still predominated (Gregory and Barnes, 1939, p. 212). Because the Alaska Fishermen's Union tended to represent nonresident cannery fishermen and other workers, disagreement over this basic issue led to a permanent split between the parent union and the local in 1950. The real fact of the matter is that Eskimo fishermen and cannery workers did not really emerge in any great importance until it was impossible for outside workers to take part in the fishery.

The Second World War brought about the increased participation of Alaskan residents in the commercial salmon fishery. During the war the scarcity of labor available in the States forced the cannery operators to draw increasingly upon resident sources of labor to meet seasonal requirements and it was only logical that the heaviest recruitment would come from the area immediately adjoining the canneries. Thus the canneries in Nushagak Bay drew heavily on the Eskimos from along the Nushagak River and in the adjacent coastal regions. However, resident recruitment also drew upon more distant Eskimo and Indian communities, from as far north as Kotzebue and Point Hope, and as far east as Minto in Alaska's interior (Hawkins and Daugherty, 1958, p. 4; Rogers, 1955, p. 5).

Following the war, there seems to have been a partial return to the former reliance upon outside labor sources, but the proportion of residents continued greater than before the war. In the Nushagak fishing district it seems to have continued at about the wartime level. The Pacific American Fisheries cannery at Dillingham, for example, employed increasing proportions of residents during the years 1943-1945 and by 1945 all employees were residents except for a few key personnel. The cannery has continued to rely upon residents for all but these few key positions (Rogers, 1955, p. 8).

An important factor that helped to increase the use of resident cannery workers after the war was the many modern airfields that were constructed throughout Alaska. These made it possible for native cannery workers to be brought in easily and rapidly from previously isolated areas (Conover, 1947, p. 7). In addition to the PAF cannery at Dillingham, the cannery at Ekuk on Nushagak Bay also pioneered the use of all-native crews. Probably not until the late 1940's did the principle of all-native cannery crews become common practice in Bristol Bay (Anonymous, 1948, p. 51).

As the number of resident independent fishermen increased, the problem arose as to how these individuals were to bargain with the industry without violating the Sherman Anti-Trust Act which prohibits independent businessmen—in this case fishermen —from grouping together to set prices. The Western Alaska Cooperative Marketing Association, established about 1954, was the answer to this problem and it bargains with the canneries to set the price paid for fish each year before the beginning of the fishing season. However, a fisherman is not required to belong to the Association, can make his separate agreement with the cannery which buys his fish, and is normally paid the price agreed upon by the industry and the marketing association. The Alaska Fishermen's Union and the Bering Sea Fishermen's Union also bargain with the industry and usually agree to accept a percentage of the price paid per fish to members of the marketing association. In 1964 and 1965 independent fishermen received $1.09 for each red salmon while the price paid to union members, who are cannery fishermen, has ranged from 69¢ to 73¢ per fish. This lower amount, of course, reflects the fact that the cannery supplies all fishing equipment to the union members.

Today Eskimos belong to all these organizations but they were much slower to participate actively as fishermen in the Nushagak River region. In fact, it was not until 1961 that they were used in even moderate numbers. Because of their inexperience, the Eskimos were frequently assigned "conversions," that is, boats which had been used with sails before power boats were allowed in Bristol Bay. These were converted to power with rebuilt sterns and often with makeshift engine installations. However, the Eskimo fishermen did well with these smaller, older, low-powered boats for which they were often charged high prices by the canneries (Anonymous, 1961, p. 23). The Nushagak River Eskimos rapidly came to participate in the fishery as independent fishermen, so much so that today few, if any, men from up the river work in the canneries. At New Koliganek, for example, in 1965 all the adult men were independent fishermen and members of the Western Alaska Cooperative Marketing Association. The point has been reached where members of the two unions almost all come from outside the Bristol Bay area. Some local fishermen belong, however, in order to obtain spring and fall work in the canneries in a maintenance capacity.

For the Nushagak River region the salmon canning and fishing industry has been the principal source of employment and income since the turn of the century even though Eskimo participation was slow to develop. In a general sense, the industry's outstanding characteristics have been a highly seasonal nature, development and ownership by interests outside Alaska, and utilization of nonresidents to meet most of the labor needs throughout the greater part of its history. Poorly planned regulation of the industry plus complicated biological factors have resulted in a steady deterioration of the resource base. However, as Rogers has pointed out, even though the total income from the fishery has declined, a larger percentage of it is being distributed to residents than at any time in the past, even in the days of the big packs (Rogers, 1955, p. 9). From the Eskimo standpoint, canneries have played an important part in the conditions of contact and have given historical depth to the acculturation process. There would seem to be few areas in Alaska where face to face interaction with whites is more intensive, particularly during the summer months. The effect of the canneries on traditional subsistence activities is another important aspect of culture change and will be discussed in detail in a later chapter.

V

Mining and Reindeer Herding

LIKE THE KOSKOKWIM, THE NUSHAGAK RIVER HAS NEVER PLAYED AN important part in the mining history of Alaska. No major stampedes were ever recorded for the river and the Nushagak was never an access route to any important goldfields. And yet, like the rest of Alaska, the Nushagak has been prospected hopefully from time to time by miners who thought that someday it might produce a strike of major proportions.

The first attempt at placer mining in the region, as noted in Chapter I, seems to have taken place along the Mulchatna River on a cut bar near the mouth of Kakhtul River in 1887-1888. In that year a party of prospectors came down the Yukon, crossed to the Kuskokwim, coasted a part of the Bering Sea and Bristol Bay coast, and ascended the Nushagak and Mulchatna rivers. They found small amounts of gold but not enough to justify extensive mining operations (Spurr, 1900, pp. 95-96; Anonymous, 1921, p. 1). However, after this initial exploration the Mulchatna continued to be a site for prospecting and even for placer mining on a small scale, although no commercial placers of importance were ever located (Mertie, 1938, p. 91).

The great stampedes to the Klondike in 1898 and Nome in 1899 left a backwash of unsuccessful prospectors in Alaska, some of whom, beginning around the turn of the century, tried their luck on the Nushagak River and its tributaries. However, as early as August of 1900, John Schoechert, Moravian missionary at Carmel, tried to discourage miners from prospecting up the Nushagak and

83

he ridiculed all stories about good strikes and rich finds; ". . . not $20 worth of gold has been taken out of the Nushagak or its tributaries" (SPG Proceedings, 1900, p. 52). A number of very small stampedes took place in the area around 1900 without much success. Shortly after this a headwater tributary of the Nushagak, known locally as Caribou Creek, north of the area covered by this study, is said to have been the site of small-scale gold placer mining and some coarse gold was also found in the upper valley of the King Salmon River in 1907 (Mertie, 1938, p. 91).

Most mining activity in the region after 1900 centered in the Mulchatna drainage. A government report on placer mining in Alaska in 1903 notes that gold had not yet been found on the Mulchatna in workable quantities but that a man could make from $4.00 to $5.00 a day working placers (Brooks, 1904, p. 48). A similar report for 1909 actually discusses routes into the Mulchatna country from Iliamna Lake and Lake Clark and mentions that there were sixteen men in the region during the summer of 1909 six of whom planned to remain during the winter. In the fall of 1909 a number of miners organized the Mulchatna mining precinct and elected a recorder, though there was a United States Commissioner and recording office at Iliamna whose district included the Mulchatna. This information was obtained by the first survey party to visit the region in the summer of 1909, and the party further reported that, on the Mulchatna upriver from the mouth of the Kakhtul, fine flour gold could be found on all the river bars (Katz, 1910, pp. 201-202).

Increasing interest in the Mulchatna area is reflected by the fact that in 1909 a company known as the Mulchatna Development Company was formed in Seattle to open the region. Their original plans included the operation of a sternwheel steamer on the river and the setting up of a trading post and sawmill. A party representing the company seems to have prospected in the area to locate a site for their post but nothing ever came of their venture. Perhaps a closer look at the Mulchatna convinced the management of the company that its steamer could never ascend the torturous river; discouraging reports from other miners may have also been a factor (Styles, 1910, pp. 132-133).

About 1912, however, reports of important discoveries of placer gold brought about a small stampede to the upper Mulchatna.

The focus of activity was in the vicinity of Bonanza Creek, a Mulchatna tributary not named on modern maps. A large number of claims were staked and some gold was recovered but again no ground that could be worked profitably was located and no serious mining has since been done in this region. However, as a result of this stampede, many men prospected the upper Mulchatna, but they left no record of their explorations (Capps, 1931, pp. 126-127).

In spite of the failure of the stampede, interest in the Mulchatna region as a promising area for prospecting continued into the 1920's. In 1921 an article in a territorial magazine gave careful directions on how to enter the upper Mulchatna country from Cook Inlet or by the way of the Kvichak River (Anonymous, 1921, p. 3). All this activity on the Mulchatna, sporadic as it was, was confined to the upper river and it is doubtful that much exploration was carried out below the mouth of the Kakhtul after 1900.

The influence prospectors exerted on the Eskimos in this general area must have been very fleeting. Since there were no permanently established mines, the people did not come into daily contact with the miners. The cabins of miners who wintered in the region were certainly visited occasionally by parties of hunters and trappers but were never enough prospectors in the region for a sufficient length of time to act as effective agents of change.

The Nushagak River region participated marginally in the Alaska reindeer industry, a program begun in 1892 among the Eskimos of Seward Peninsula and more northerly regions. The industry was one of Sheldon Jackson's innovations and it was organized with the idea of helping to put the economy of the Eskimos on a sounder footing, particularly those people along the northwest coast of Alaska who depended heavily on sea mammals for subsistence and whose food supply had been seriously decimated by commercial whalers during the last half of the nineteenth century. As early as 1896, Moravian missionaries at Bethel and Carmel asked the Bureau of Education to send them reindeer for their missions, and in 1901 a herd, numbering 176 deer, was driven from Unalakleet to the lower Kuskokwim accompanied by Lapp herders who earlier had been persuaded to come to Alaska to teach herding techniques to the Eskimos (Jackson, 1897, pp.

131-132). However, government reports that document the reindeer program are not clear as to the ultimate destination of all the deer driven to the Kuskokwim. In the annual report for 1901, the Carmel misson is listed as having received 88 deer and a separate Nushagak herd continues to be listed in the reports for 1902, 1903, and 1904. Aside from the simple listing, however, there are no other references to a Nushagak herd nor is it possible to find a reindeer herd mentioned in any of the Moravian sources (Jackson, 1903, p. 19; 1904, p. 18; 1905, p. 12).

Another version of the spread of reindeer throughout southwestern Alaska is provided by Adolf Stecker, a Moravian missionary at Bethel, who reports that in 1904 the Bureau of Education decided to transfer 300 deer from the Kuskokwim to the Copper River. The trip was begun in December of that year but the herd became stranded "at or near" Iliamna Lake and remained there. Stecker maintained that from this herd came all the herds in the Nushagak and Togiak regions (DRHA, vol. 15, pp. 150-151).

The first official report of a herd of the Nushagak occurs in 1905 and perhaps this is the most reliable source on the matter. In the spring of that year a small herd of 50 surplus males, the property of the mission, was driven to the Nushagak from Bethel. Dr. J. H. Romig was at Carmel at the time and apparently the herd was kept during the summer and most of the animals were slaughtered in the fall. Dr. Romig disposed of the meat to the canneries as an addition to their food supply and it was hoped that the procedure could be followed the next year and that ultimately reindeer would become a new source of income for the mission. However, the closing of the Carmel mission station in 1906 seems to have ended the experiment and certainly the Eskimos of the region had no contact with reindeer herding up to this time (Hamilton, 1906, p. 63; Jackson, 1906, pp. 70-71).

The subsequent history of reindeer herding in the Nushagak River region is difficult to trace because of the paucity of source material. However, the industry never played as big a part in the life of the Eskimos of this area as it did, for example, along the Kuskokwim River. In the report of the Commissioner of Education for 1909 there is reference to a reindeer herd having been established at Kogiung on the Kvichak River, and the following year new government reindeer stations appeared at Chogiung and Ugashik (Report of the Commissioner of Education. . . . 1909, pub. 1910, p. 1299; same for 1910, pub. 1911, p. 1365). In 1913 the only herd in the Nushagak area is listed as being at Chogiung and numbering 400 animals. By contrast, seven herds are listed for the Bethel area with a total of more than 6,000 deer (Report of the-Governor of Alaska. . . . 1914, pub. 1914, pp. 14-15). It seems likely that during this general period a number of Eskimos worked as herders for the government and that a few owned deer themselves. The pattern for the Kuskokwim was doubtless followed on the Nushagak to some extent with the deer becoming increasingly concentrated in the hands of whites, while the Eskimos served mainly as hired herders (Oswalt, 1963, p. 46).

In 1928 over 8,000 deer are listed in southwestern Alaska and this figure apparently does not include the Kuskokwim. At this time the native cooperative reindeer associations were said to hold the vast majority of native-owned deer but no deer are listed for the Nushagak area. This contrasts markedly to the activities of the Kuskokwim Reindeer and Trading Company at Akiak which had a herd of 30,000 animals (Report of the Governor of Alaska. . . . 1926, pub. 1926, p. 77). In the early 1930's Mertie saw small herds of deer in the Wood River Lakes region and on the Kokwok River. These were said to be native-owned (Mertie, 1938, p. 35). Informants at Ekwok reported that in 1940 there were five men living in the village who owned a total of 260 deer, but nearly half of these were the property of one man.

This is all that can be said about reindeer herding in the Nushagak River region, and by 1945 the last deer had disappeared from the area. The reasons for the disappearance are doubtless multiple and similar to those that have been noted for the industry in other parts of Alaska: poor herding techniques, predation, disease, marketing problems, and vacillating government policies. The nomadic routine required for good close herding scarcely fitted in with the sedentary pattern of village life traditional to all Alaskan Eskimos. Failure on the part of the government to appreciate this fact was probably the single most important reason for the eventual complete failure of the reindeer herding program (see Oswalt, 1963, pp. 45 47; Lantis, 1952; VanStone, 1962b, pp. 26-27).

Participation by the Eskimos of the Nushagak River region in the program was always marginal. Perhaps the influence of the canneries and the tendency for the people to congregate on the coast during the summer months was partly responsible for this. Another factor may have been the Moravians' decision to close their mission at the critical moment when deer were being introduced into the region. The Moravians were always interested in the program and frequently talked about the good pasturage in the region. At any rate the program cannot be considered a major instrument of culture change and today little, if anything, beyond a few abandoned corrals reminds an onlooker that reindeer herding commanded the time and interest of the local inhabitants.

VI

Educational and Medical Services

◇◆

THE HISTORY OF FORMAL EDUCATION IN THE NUSHAGAK RIVER REGION is so intimately connected with the history of the missions that discussing the two aspects of culture change separately introduces a slight distortion. This distortion can be minimized if the reader bears in mind that the educational services introduced and offered by the Russian Orthodox Church and, later, the Moravian Church were an integral part of their efforts to intoduce the concepts of Christianity, but that they formed, at the same time, the base on which secular education in the area was to develop.

Indications are that an educational program at Alexandrovski Redoubt was contemplated as early as 1838. In that year, Gregory Golovin, Veniaminov's successor as clergyman of the Unalaska church, visited the redoubt and suggested to Fedore Kolmakov that the latter's son Konstantin give basic instruction in reading and writing to boys living at or near the post. The elder Kolmakov received permission from I. A. Kuprianov, then general manager of the Russian-American Company, to purchase a house in which to lodge the students and hold classes. Kuprianov also agreed to send primers and copybooks but at the same time he warned Kolmakov that instruction was to be given only to those who showed ability and at times that would not conflict with Company activities. The general manager further emphasized that the young men should not be "diverted in vain through teaching" which "is not as much needed nor as useful as are their native occupations."

Whether Konstantin Kolmakov actually organized and taught the classes is not known (Russian-American Company Records: Communications Sent, vol. 16, no. 466, folios 176-177).

Little information exists concerning the first official school at Alexandrovski Redoubt that was opened at the time the mission was established in 1842, and our knowledge of educatonal facilities at the post during all the years of the Russian period is sketchy. Father Veniaminov, writing to the Metropolitan, Philaret, in 1849, mentions that the Eskimos living near the mission willingly sent their children to the mission school and that there were 24 students in 1848 who were referred to as being "in the service of the missionary." Apparently even adults were eager to learn to read and write (Barsukov, 1887-1888, vol. 1, p. 222). Veniaminov's statements imply that the mission school was for Eskimo children but apparently this was not always the case. In 1864 the Nushagak school is spoken of as being specifically for children of mixed blood with the priest, in addition to the regular school, frequently calling the children to his home for Christian instruction (DRHA, vol. 1, p. 148). Whether the school operated continuously between 1849 and 1864 is not known. Presumably in these early years the educational program of the Nushagak mission was considered peripheral to other mission activities and may have depended to a large extent on the interests of the priests and the extent to which children could be persuaded to attend.

The next reference to the Nushagak school occurs in 1877 when the priest apparently began instruction on his own initiative, which suggests that no school was held for a number of years previous to this date. In this year Eskimo children were taught Russian and church singing by the priest and song leader, presumably Vasili Shiskin and Vasili Orlov. School was open from September 1 to February 1; after this date the Eskimos normally took their families to hunt and trap in the interior. School hours were from nine in the morning until three in the afternoon with primers and brief catechisms the only textbooks. Average daily attendance was 15 boys and 7 girls. The priest mentions that his students worked hard but their progress was slow because they did not use the Russian language at home. In addition to the school, Father Shishkin also held afternoon classes for adults between

September 1, 1878, and March 1, 1879. At these classes moral and religious instruction was given and there was singing (DRHA, vol. 1, p. 331). In 1881 and 1882 Deacon Orlov was teaching school and in addition offering a religious class three times a week for adults (DRHA, vol. 2, p. 144).

In spite of the scarcity of source material, it seems safe to assume that the educational services of the Orthodox mission at Nushagak before 1885 were at best desultory. Classes were held sporadically and the subject matter taught was very limited. Presumably when the priest and his assistant were away from Nushagak no school at all was held, and even under the most favorable circumstances long gaps during the year when no classes were conducted. When the Moravian mission and school at Carmel were established in 1886, the Orthodox mission was forced by the competition to intensify its educational offerings. After 1886 the source material on education increases greatly because during its early years the Moravian school operated with a grant from the United States government and annual statements appear in government reports as well as in the publications of the Moravian Church.

The Moravians had been encouraged to establish their missions in southwestern Alaska by Sheldon Jackson. It was his explicit wish that schools would be established. In the case of Nushagak, plans for an industrial school preceded other mission plans and a grant of $1,500 was obtained from the Bureau of Education for the purpose of setting up this school (SPG Proceedings, 1886, pp. 4-5). And in the summer of 1887 Mr. and Mrs. F. E. Wolff and Miss Mary Huber arrived at the mouth of the Nushagak River to open the school and mission.

The school opened in January of 1888 with 9 pupils and almost immediately that number increased to 21. The attendance seems to have aroused Father Shishkin's jealousy and thus began the feud between the two missions that lasted until the Moravians abandoned the Nushagak area in 1906. In 1887 the Orthodox school at Nushagak, one of seventeen in Alaska supported by the Russian government, had an average daily attendance of 8. At that time the Russians were operating their schools with an annual appropriation of $20,000 which was in addition to the $40,000 annual appropriation to support the various Orthodox churches in the territory (Report of the Governor of Alaska. . . . 1887, pub. 1887, pp. 27-28). The Nushagak priest would not allow the people to send their children to the new Moravian school. The Russian priests attempted to frighten the children by telling them that if they learned English, the American government would carry them off to San Francisco and make soldiers of them. The harassment of the children was apparently so great that, if the Moravian reports are to be believed, whenever Shishkin or Orlov came to Kanulik and passed the Carmel schoolhouse, some of the pupils ducked their heads below the windowsill while others tried to hide. To encourage the children in their attendance, and to attempt to counteract the efforts of the priest, the school furnished two substantial meals every day (Report of the Commissioner of Education. . . . 1887-1888, pub. 1889, p. 186).

The Moravians noted that those who were regular in their attendance at school made good progress. However, from the beginning the problem of attendance—whether it was attributable to the opposition of the Orthodox priest or simply the result of the Eskimos' failure to understand the role of the school and the necessity of regular attendance—was the greatest obstacle. The government realized this problem and speculated on the advisability of establishing a home school to attract orphans and those who might come from distant villages if they were promised food and shelter. The Carmel missionaries began to make plans to board these pupils and speculated that since the canneries drew large numbers of Eskimos to the coast, the area could become an important center for a school. Moreover, the Moravians were shocked at the physical condition of their pupils, many of whom came to school covered with vermin, and felt that the children could be educated, civilized, and Christianized only if they were living at the school (SPG Proceedings, 1888, pub. 1888, p. 29; Report of the Commissioner of Education. . . . 1887-1888, pub. 1889, p. 186).

The first school year at Carmel closed on May 9, 1888, because the fishing season was beginning and it was useless to try to keep the children in school (SPG Proceedings, 1888, pub. 1888, p. 29). School reopened on the twenty-seventh of August, with a grant of $1,000 from the United States government and an increased enrollment that totaled 25 at its highest point. A large barabara had been constructed to house children from Nushagak, Togiak, and other neighboring villages. These children were allowed to go home on Fridays, returning to school on the following Monday mornings. Most students were working on what were called "primary charts" which apparently indicates beginners. A few were also working on first, second, third, and fourth readers. Spelling, English, arithmetic, drawing, writing, and sewing were the subjects taught (Report of the Commissioner of Education. . . . 1888-1889, pub. 1891, vol. 2, pp. 756-757, 760-761). In the school year 1889-1890 the highest enrollment was 31, but opposition from the Orthodox mission was again strong the following year and no more than 18 pupils were in attendance at any one time. The success in 1889-1890 probably stemmed, at least in part from the fact that the priest and Mr. Clark, Alaska Commercial Company manager who also seems to have opposed the Moravians, were in San Francisco. On his return, Father Shishkin is described as increasing his persecution of families that sent their children to school (SPG Proceedings, 1891, pub. 1891, p. 28). The Moravians reported that many parents expressed a desire to send their children but were afraid to do so. A protest, endorsed by the officers of the Moravian Missionary Society, was sent to the Bureau of Education and the captain of the Coast Guard cutter *Bear* was instructed to visit the Nushagak and make a personal inquiry. However, various circumstances prevented this visit (Report of the Commissioner of Education. . . . 1890-1891, pub. 1894, vol. 2, pp. 928-929, 934-935).

These reports of relations between the two missions come exclusively from the Moravians and doubtless present a rather one-sided account of the controversy. In the few Russian sources for this period that it has been possible to examine, not one reference is made to the Moravians. Very likely both sides exhibited provocative behavior, and it should be remembered that, after all, the Moravians were intruders in an area long considered by the Orthodox Church to be its sphere of influence. In this connection it is interesting to note that the enumerator of the Eleventh Census, in summing up the matter—incidentally one of the few comments on the whole affair by a presumably disinterested outsider —wryly commented that the Russian priest "fails to discriminate between the government teacher and a rival missionary represented by the same individual" (Porter, 1893, p. 190). It is possible to appreciate Father Shishkin's inability to make this distinction.

It is perhaps worthwhile at this point to evaluate the progress made by the Moravian school during the first five years of its existence. Although enrollment figures are probably inaccurate and often conflicting, the school was attracting a solid core of boarding students even though the attendance of local children fluctuated considerably. In the summer of 1890 lumber was shipped from San Francisco for the construction of a larger schoolhouse and dormitory facilities (Hamilton, 1890, p. 20; Porter, 1893, pp. 96-97). Probably the school was fulfilling a definite need since, even in response to competition, it is unlikely that the Orthodox mission extended its educational work much beyond the desultory instruction of children of the clergy and a few mixed-bloods (Porter, 1893, p. 190). The Moravians made up for their failure to attract students from Nushagak and Kanulik by successfully obtaining pupils from interior villages. That the Moravians were encouraged by their efforts at this time is attested to by the comments of Bishop Bachman during his inspection tour of Alaska in the summer of 1891. After visiting Carmel and talking with the missionaries, he wrote the following in his report of the trip:

> The hope of the mission lies pre-eminently in the school and this is bound to win the confidence and support of the natives more and more, as the utter worthlessness of the opposing Greek establishment becomes more clearly apparent. As the teachers learn how to deal with the natives in order to secure the best results, the fame of the school will surely spread; and its location is such that more than sufficient scholars to fill it can be secured in time from the northern coast of the peninsula, and the scattered villages on Bristol Bay and the Igushik River (SPG Proceedings, 1891, pub. 1891, pp. 77-78).

The Carmel school received no funds from the United States government after 1894 as all contract school arrangements were abolished in the following year (see Jenness, 1962). In spite of this, in 1895-1896 the school is spoken of as being so attractive that all applicants for boarding status could not be accepted. The missionaries mentioned that it was almost impossible to retain the girls past the age of thirteen or fourteen at which age their par-

ents expected them to marry (Report of the Commissioner of
Education. . . . 1895-1896, pub. 1897, vol. 2, p. 1443). Relations
between the two missions continued to be bad as the following
exchange of letters, which took place in late March, 1896, illustrates:

To Rev. J. H. Schoechert
Dear Sir:
 As there are many children going to your public school which
have been christened in the Russian Greek Church I would beg
you to let all such ones visit the church in which they were
christened during Holy Week. I presume that you can let them go
on Saturday or Sunday or any time that will not interfere with their
school duties(.) (A)t any convenient time please inform me and I
will send a responsible man who will convey them to Nushagak
and back again to you. Awaiting your kind attention. I remain
Yours very sincerely
Rev. V. V. Modestov

p.s. In case you feel disinclined to let them come to Nushagak
please give me permission to administer the Holy Sacraments to
them at your mission.

To which the Rev. Mr. Schoechert replied:

Mr. V. V. Modestov
Dear Sir:
 In regards to your request I can but say that such children which
attend our daily Public School—not boarders—can go to your daily
services any time. But such which attend the mission school cannot
go neither can you come up here to administer the Holy Sacraments. This is in accordance with the rules of the Government and
the direct request of the ex-Governor of Alaska while he visited here.
Very respectfully yours
Moravian Mission, Carmel, Alaska
Rev. J. H. Schoechert, Pres.
(Alaska Records, 1892-1938)

The reference to a visit by a former governor of Alaska refers to
A. P. Swineford's inspection tour of the Territory in the summer
of 1888, during which he visited both Nushagak and Carmel.
 By 1902 the conflict between the two missions concerning the
school seems to have cooled, largely because children of members
of the Russian Orthodox Church had ceased to attend by that

time. Again the orphan children who were under the care of the mission could be relied upon to attend school regularly. Others might attend for a while but when the novelty wore off, they preferred to stay away and play. In the annual report of the Commissioner of Education for 1901 the Carmel school is referred to for the first time as a public school, presumably meaning that the government had assumed full responsiblity for its maintenance. A member of the mission staff continued to teach, however, until the spring of 1904 when the first government teacher was sent to Carmel because the mission was shorthanded (Report of the Commissioner of Education. . . . 1901, pub. 1902, vol. 2, p. 1465; same for 1902, pub. 1903, vol. 2, p. 1230; SPG Proceedings, 1904, pub. 1904, p. 15).

The seeming success which the Carmel school was enjoying and its ability to overcome the difficulties which it faced from inception little prepares us for Bishop Hamilton's cool evaluation, made when he visited Carmel in 1905. The Bishop expressed doubt as to the permanent value of the school. Only a few of the former students, he said, were a credit to the people who had educated them. Some had even accepted positions as assistants to the Orthodox priest, presumably having, in the bishop's mind, been bribed by the $35.00 a month salary. He further noted that only seven of the former boarding students were still members of the Moravian Church. Bishop Hamilton's evaluation of the school apparently was based largely on his interpretation of its value to the mission. At any rate, he was probably influenced at that time by his contemplated decision to abandon missionary activity on the Nushagak (Hamilton, 1906, p. 35).

The fate of the Carmel school following the abandonment of the mission is not absolutely clear, but there is no certain indication that it was closed. The report of the Commissioner of Education for 1906 lists a school as having been established at Nushagak in the fall of 1905 although no details are given. In the same year or the next the first school on the west side of the bay seems to have been launched in cannery buildings at "Dillingham," probably the Bradford cannery at what is now called Kanakanak (Report of the Commissioner of Education. . . . 1906, pub. 1907, vol. 1, pp. 239, 241; same for 1907, pub. 1908, vol. 1, p. 279). One of the first school teachers at the Nushagak school was Dr. J. H.

Romig, the former Moravian missionary at Bethel and Carmel. After severing his official connection with the Moravian Church in 1905, Romig lived on the west coast for a while, returning to Alaska in 1908. In the annual report of the Governor of Alaska for 1908, Romig is listed as the teacher at Nushagak and at this time the school appears to have been maintained, or at least supported in part, by the Territory of Alaska. It was definitely not a Bureau of Education school (Report of the Governor of . . . Alaska. . . . 1908, pub. 1908, p. 26). The school at Carmel presumably continued to be wholly supported by the federal bureau.

During the summer of 1908 an official of the Bureau of Education made his annual inspection of the federally supported schools and visited the Nushagak Bay region to inspect the two schools at Carmel and Dillingham. However, he broadened the scope of his inquiry in order to ascertain the educational needs of the people and has left some interesting comments on the Eskimos of the region which may or may not be exaggerated. In talking with people in unspecified places in the area he was shocked to discover that they had no knowledge of the United States government and believed themselves still under the rule of Russia. When the official spoke about a school, "several of the villages asked for a Russian school, and only after some argument and after they learned that the priest was favorably disposed, were they inclined to favor the establishment of schools whose instruction would be in English" (Report of the Commissioner of Education. . . . 1908, pub. 1909, vol. 2, p. 1045). It is not known what villages are referred to here and it is probably also necessary to make allowances for the civil servant in a strange and remote environment.[*] Nevertheless, his comments suggest that in spite of the canneries, missionaries, and other agents of contact, culture change in the Nushagak River region was progressing very slowly.

In 1909 Dr. Romig was appointed district superintendent of schools for southwestern Alaska and continued to headquarter at Nushagak. During the summer of 1909 school buildings were constructed at Kanakanak and Chogiung, the latter being the Eskimo village at the site of the present community of Dillingham (Report of the Commissioner of Education. . . . 1908, pub. 1909, vol. 2, p. 1026; same for 1909, pub. 1910, vol. 2, p. 1299; Anonymous, 1920a, p. 7).

From this time, information on the development of educational facilities in the Nushagak River region is confined almost entirely to occasional listings in government reports which refer to the opening of new schools or the construction of new buildings. Much of this information is difficult to follow because of the confusing nomenclature of communities in Nushagak Bay. There is some reason to believe that 1914 was the last year in which a Russian church school was operated at Nushagak, or at least the last year in which any kind of records were kept. Presumably the priest still instructed the young members of his church, but secular education had won the day (DRHA, vol. 2, p. 345). A new territorial school was in operation at Dillingham during 1920-1921 and in 1922 preliminary steps were taken to convert the orphanage that had been established at Kanakanak to care for the orphans of the 1918-1919 influenza epidemic into an industrial school for southwestern Alaska. This was done in 1924 and the school was operated until 1932 (Report of the Governor of Alaska. . . . 1922, pub. 1922, p. 64; same for 1923, pub. 1923, p. 46; same for 1932, pub. 1932, p. 95). The territorial school at Nushagak seems to have been closed in 1930 and may not have opened again until the fall of 1946 (Report of the Governor of Alaska. . . . 1931, pub. 1931, p. 93; Anonymous, 1947, p. 27).

In 1930 a colony of Seventh Day Adventists established a small settlement at the extreme southeast end of Lake Aleknagik, a community that came to be called Aleknagik. A school was started almost immediately but there is no evidence that it became a territorial school until 1945 or 1946. This school would have served the growing Eskimo population of Aleknagik and must be thought of as one of the first educational facilities provided for the people of the Nushagak River region exclusive of Nushagak Bay (Anonymous, 1941, p. 19; Annual Report of the Governor of Alaska. . . . 1946, n.d., p. 18). A Bureau of Indian Affairs school was constructed at Ekwok in 1932, and classes began there the following year. This was the first school on the Nushagak River, and it was turned over to the Territory in 1954 (Annual Report of the Governor of Alaska. . . . 1932, pub. 1932, p. 94). Bureau of Indian Affairs schools were established at Koliganek (later New Koliganek) and New Stuyahok in 1954 and at Portage Creek in 1963. The government may have been slow to build schools at these three points because of the fluctuating population of the river and the tendencies of the villages to shift at relatively frequent intervals. For example, the people of New Stuyahok, a community that was not founded much before 1940, requested a school in the early 1950's and were told that if they built one themselves, they would be given a teacher and books. If they showed that they intended to remain permanently settled at New Stuyahok, the Bureau would ten consider building them a school. A fine new building was constructed at that community in 1961.

In concluding this brief survey of the development of educational services in the Nushagak River region, it might be well to keep in mind that although some facilities have been available in this area as long as in most other parts of Alaska, the number of people who were in a position to take advantage of these facilities was relatively small. In the Dillingham region today there is a small group of educated mixed-bloods who were educated by the schools in Nushagak Bay at the turn of the century. Allowing for the fact that this must be, of necessity, a dwindling group today, it is still possible to note that a vast majority of the people of the region were largely untouched by any kind of education until after the end of the Second World War. This contrasts markedly with coastal regions, and even some interior areas, further to the north.

The early history of contact in southwestern Alaska records the rapid spread of introduced diseases, decimating a population that had never built up an immunity to them. The first reported epidemic in the Nushagak River region occured sometime prior to 1832 when it was mentioned in a report sent by F. P. Wrangell to the main office of the Russian-American Company in St. Petersburg. There was no mention of the number of dead, but it was said to have been "considerable" (Russian-American Company Records: Communications Sent, vol. 9, no. 460, folios 345-346). In 1838-1839 smallpox swept the Kuskokwim and Nushagak river regions, but figures on fatalities are conflicting. According to Tikhmenev, more than 500 people were infected; of these 200 died. I. A. Kuprianov, in his report to St. Petersburg, listed 552 deaths as having been recounted to him by Fedor Kolmakov at Alexandrovski Redoubt. Kolmakov's figures may be more accurate since they were based on accounts from Eskimos visiting the redoubt and from his son, Petr, who was traveling on the Kuskokwim at the time. Among those who died, Kolmakov mentioned ten "honorable *toyons*," all having silver medals (Tikhmenev, 1939-1940, pt. II, pp. 266, 388; Russian-American Company Records: Communications Sent, vol. 16, no. 479, folio 187). In February of 1838 vaccinations were administered for the first time to the residents of Alexandrovski and other villages in the area in an attempt to check the epidemic, but it was still raging as late as September, 1839 (Russian-American Company Records: Communications Sent, vol. 15, no. 244, folios 314-315; vol. 17, no. 444, folio 425). The following year more people were vaccinated (Browning, 1962, p. 37). Although epidemics similar to this one may have been relatively rare, there is every indication that once European diseases had been introduced, they took a yearly toll that was not only great in terms of numbers of dead, but that greatly weakened the resistance of the survivors. In the many years of sickness, a few stand out as epidemic years, but the specter of ill health and death was continually present among the Eskimo population of all southwestern Alaska.

The fearful toll taken by the introduced diseases served, in many cases, to make the work of the missionaries more difficult. Writing in 1863, Hieromonk Theophil noted how he had asked the people in one of the Nushagak River villages why they were reluctant to adopt Christianity and received the following answer:

> Before the Russians came here our people lived to a ripe old age, now hardly anybody attains it. Formerly we did not know about epidemics but since we started to baptize our children and be baptized, scarcely a year passes without some kind of epidemic and deaths.

When Theophil countered that the Russians also were baptized and yet suffered no ill effects, the Eskimos insisted that the Russians had built up an immunity against the ill effects of baptism (DRHA, vol. 2, p. 137). Those Eskimos who did not subscribe to the germ theory of baptism believed that the Russians wished to exterminate them and therefore put some kind of poison into the communion cup (DRHA, vol. 2, p. 138).

The next reported epidemic did not take place until 1886, but it can easily be imagined that there were many years in between when illness raged unchecked through the Eskimo population with no one to discribe the details. The 1886 epidemic of pulmonary diseases was noted by the Moravians (Report of the Governor of Alaska. . . . 1887, pub. 1887, p. 34) and subsequent reports are filled with references to illness. In 1899-1900 a major epidemic of influenza and measles struck and the people tended to blame it on the Twelfth Census, statistics for which were being collected at the time. This is the epidemic that old residents of the Kuskokwim and Nushagak regions refer to today as the "great sickness." At Carmel every child under the age of two died and the Orthodox Church listed 111 deaths among its parishoners in 1899, about four times the usual number (SPG Proceedings, 1899, pub. 1899, p. 23; Schwalbe, 1951, p. 60; DRHA, vol. 2, p. 331; Report of the Commissioner of Education. . . . 1898-1899, pub. 1900, vol. 2, pp. 1394-1395). Famine followed in the wake of this epidemic, for the people were too weak and sick during the summer months to gather food supplies for winter. Even during the summer of 1902, Osgood noted that the Eskimos he encountered along the Nushagak River were in a very destitute condition and many were suffering from the effects of disease (Osgood, 1904, p. 18).

In the summer of 1904 the Moravian medical missionary, Dr. J. H. Romig, and his wife came to Carmel. Dr. Romig was the first medical practitioner to settle on the Nushagak and the Moravians thought he could help broaden their service and perhaps retrieve some of their waning influence in the region. Dr. Romig had offered to come as a medical missionary and he proposed to maintain a small hospital in the mission buildings from which he could serve not only the Eskimos but whites and others who were employed during the summer months in the canneries. It was felt that the presence and practice of a medical missionary would be one of the most effective ways of placing the shifting population of Nushagak Bay under permanent religious influence. With this in mind, the Carmel station was equipped with a small medical annex that would have a separate medical and financial existence under Dr. Romig's direction. The enterprise was to be conducted as an experiment during the first year at the expense of the mission. If the plan was successful, Dr. Romig would reimburse the church. The doctor doubtless hoped to build up a lucrative private practice among cannery workers and those Euro-Americans who remained in the country throughout the year as watchmen for the canneries, independent traders, and trappers. At the same time the Moravian Church thought that a "home mission" might be established which would in time become self-supporting with the aid of hospital receipts. In this way the struggling mission among the Eskimos might eventually be merged in a "home mission" for evangelistic work among the churchless white population and thus enlarge the sphere of the mission as a center of Christian influence (SPG Proceedings, 1904, pub. 1904, pp. 15-16; Schwalbe, 1951, p. 61; Hamilton, 1906, p. 36; Report of the Commissioner of Education. . . . 1903, pub. 1905, vol. 2, p. 2358).

The new venture was begun in the summer of 1904 but after more than a year Dr. Romig found that his expectations were not realized and decided against continuing the experiment. The Moravians were reimbursed for the money advanced and Dr. Romig withdrew from missionary service. The canneries had not been interested in the project because many of them had their own doctors who accompanied their ships north in summer. The few permanent white residents of the area were apathetic and apparently the Eskimos did not understand the nature of the services that were being offered and did not take advantage of them (SPG Proceedings, 1906, pub. 1906, pp. 82-83; Hamilton, 1906, p. 36; Schwalbe, 1951, p. 62).

In 1908 Dr. Romig returned to the Nushagak, purchased the Moravian mission buildings, and used them for offices and a small hospital. In 1908 he also contracted with the Bureau of Education to furnish medical relief to the Eskimos of Nushagak and vicinity and to make occasional tours along the coast of Bristol Bay as far west as Togiak and southward to Ugashik. His appointment as district superintendent of schools for southwestern Alaska in 1909 widened the sphere of his medical work to include all of southwestern Alaska (SPG Proceedings, 1906, pub. 1906, p. 14; Report of the Commissioner of Education. . . . 1908, pub. 1909, vol. 2, p. 1026; Hawkins and Dougherty, 1958, p. 4).

How long Dr. Romig stayed at Carmel is not known definitely, but it cannot have been very long, for in the summer of 1911 a hospital was established at Nushagak under the management of Dr. L. H. French. The annual report of the Commissioner of Education for 1911 suggests that this was the only medical facility in the area, so it would seem that Dr. Romig did not maintain his hospital at Carmel for more than two years. However, it is always difficult to interpret the government publications with regard to specific locations in the Nushagak Bay area. Frequently they simply use the term "Nushagak" when the Nushagak village is not meant at all, but some other part of the bay (Report of the Commissioner of Education. . . . 1911, pub. 1912, vol. 2, p. 1381). The Bureau of Education hospital at Nushagak—if indeed it was at Nushagak—was definitely maintained as late as 1915 and a medical doctor stationed at that location is mentioned in reports of the governor of Alaska until 1925 (Report of the Governor of Alaska. . . . 1915, pub. 1915, p. 29; same for 1925, pub. 1925, p. 88).

Perhaps the most serious period of illness ever to occur in the Nushagak River region was the influenza epidemic of the fall of 1918 and the spring of 1919 which was very serious in many parts of Alaska, just as it had been nearly a year earlier in the United States. The Moravians at Bethel reported that 200 people, whites and Eskimos alike, had died in the Nushagak Bay region. Older people at Dillingham and along the river vividly recall the terrible mortality of this period. Every person in the large villages of Igushik and Kanakanak either died or moved away. Only 8 persons are said to have survived at Chogiung. Many small villages in the bay and along the river were either wiped out or abandoned at this time. The few survivors frequently moved from a place which had been the scene of intense misery and death. The situation is vividly described in a small pamphlet issued by the Alaska Packers Association. When the Association's vessels arrived in the bay in the middle of May, 1919, most of the population was sick and even those who were not ill were sitting in their cold houses waiting for death. The most violent period of the spring epidemic seems to have been short, lasting from about the middle of May to the middle of June. The doctor accompanying the Alaska Packers Association ships offered medical assistance to as many people as he could, and out of the 100 people who received direct or indirect treatment, 34 died. Bronchial pneumonia is mentioned as being the cause of the greater number of deaths and pulmonary tuberculosis frequently developed from the original disease. The doctor also noted that the sick often gave up all hope and sometimes refused both food and medical treatment (Anonymous, n.d., pp. 21, 25). This epidemic was probably the single most important factor affecting contemporary settlement patterns in the Nushagak River region.

During 1918 the Bureau of Education building at Kanakanak, erected as a school in 1909, was enlarged and remodeled as a hospital. This was apparently the first hospital on the west side of Nushagak Bay (Report of the Commissioner of Education. . . . 1918, pub. 1918, p. 143). The following year construction was begun on an orphanage to care for the orphans created by the influenza epidemic. It was completed and ready for occupancy by the fall of 1920. The orphange buildings were eventually converted for use as an industrial school (Report of the Governor of Alaska. . . . 1920, pub. 1920, p. 62; Anonymous, 1920b, p. 31).

Some form of medical service was permanently established in the Nushagak River region from this time on and the Kanakanak hospital, now associated with the Alaska Native Health Service, Department of Indian Health, United States Public Health Service, has always been the center of these services. However, as late as 1925 the vast area of the interior from the lower reaches of the Nushagak River to the Yukon had, with few exceptions, never been visited by a physician. Efforts were made to secure funds for a survey of the country to determine whether the many epidemics in that great region were really diseases caused by contagion or simply food anaphylaxis due to seasonal changes in diet (Report of the Governor of Alaska. . . . 1925, pub. 1925, p. 76).

In 1932 fire destroyed the small Kanakanak hospital and it was replaced with a thirty-two bed unit in 1940. Nine years later a tuberculosis custodial unit was added. The services, as well as the facilities, also improved. Field nursing activities were extended to the Bristol Bay area in 1939 and dental facilities were established at the Kanakanak hospital in 1952 (Annual Report of the Secretary of the Interior. . . . 1940, pub. 1940, p. 400; same for 1949, pub. 1949, p. 352; Annual Report of the Governor of Alaska. . . . 1939, pub. 1939, p. 52; same for 1952, pub. 1952, p. 81).

Today the services of the Kanakanak Department of Indian

Health installation are available to the entire Nushagak River region. Regularly scheduled monthly clinics are held at the Nushagak River communities of New Stuyahok, Ekwok, New Koliganek, and Portage Creek as well as in many other villages in the Bristol Bay region. At the time of these visits by the medical officer in charge of the Kanakanak hospital, pre- and postnatal clinics are held, along with well baby clinics; there are also school physical examinations, and general medical care. Public Health nursing services are provided for Department of Indian Health beneficiaries through a contract with the Alaska Department of Health and Welfare, Division of Health. A public health nurse is stationed at Dillingham and she visits all the villages in the region to conduct a generalized program that includes therapeutic, preventive, and educational activities (Anonymous, 1960, pp. 4-6).

Medical services, while relatively recent in the Nushagak River region compared with other agents of change discussed in this study, have nevertheless had a considerable impact on the inhabitants, an impact that is out of proportion to the length of time the people have been exposed to Western medicine. This may be due to the experience that the Eskimos have had with introduced European diseases, an experience that has taught them to accept strange treatment of strange illnesses from outsiders. Whatever the reason, the monthly clinics in the villages are well attended and modern methods of baby care are, in particular, adhered to by the majority of Eskimo mothers. The fact that nearly all the Eskimos in the region spend their summers on Nushagak Bay, puts them in close touch with the hospital and with the public health nurse.

PART TWO

Emerging Socioeconomic Patterns

VII

Population Groupings and Settlement
Patterns in the Nineteenth
and Early Twentieth Centuries

◆◆◆

BEFORE WE DEAL WITH EMERGING SOCIOECONOMIC PATTERNS IN THE
Nushagak River region, it is necessary to say something about the
subcultural affiliation of those Eskimos in the area at the time of
first Russian penetration. As noted in the introduction, this question cannot be disposed of in a sentence or two, as it could in
many other parts of Alaska, because of the many population shifts
that have characterized the area from the time of the earliest records to the present.

Possibly the first written statements concerning subcultural
groupings in the Nushagak River region were contained in the
journals of members of the Korsakovski expedition and are reported by Berkh (1823, p. 47). The inhabitants of Bristol Bay in
the region of the mouth of the Nushagak River are referred to as
"Glakmiut," but no additional details are given except that these
people were constantly at war with the inhabitants of the Kuskokwim River. Khromchenko was apparently the first to make a distinction between the coastal Eskimos and those who inhabited
the Nushagak River. He refers to the people in the Nushagak Bay
area as "Aglegmiut," presumably the Glakmiut of Korsakovski.
The Nushagak River people are spoken of as being distinct from

those Eskimos living around the shores of the bay and are called "Kiatagmiut."

Khromchenko and his party visited the mouth of the Nushagak River during the summers of 1821 and 1822. Seven years later Vasiliev, as reported by Zagoskin (1956, p. 215), made the same distinction between coastal and interior peoples and supplied the additional information that the term Kiatagmiut, which he used not only to refer to the people of the Nushagak River but also of Nushagak (Tikchik) Lake, means "inhabitants of the upper river," a translation verified by informants today. The Aglegmiut, according to Vasiliev, occupied Bristol Bay and some of the neighboring interior lakes. Veniaminov, in his writings, seems to have followed the Khromchenko-Vasiliev classification, although he frequently refers to the Kiatagmiut as "Kiatents" or "Kiatentsi" (Barsukov, 1886-1888, vol. 2, p. 42; 1897-1901, vol. 1, pp. 17, 222, 372-373). Wrangell, writing in 1839, suggested that the Aglegmiut also occupied the mouth of the Naknek River, while the Kiatagmiut lived along the Nushagak and Ilgajak riverbanks. This latter river, which Wrangell believed to be the Mulchatna, is, as we have already noted, almost certainly the Ilgayak of Zagoskin (1956, map) and thus in reality is the upper Nushagak (Wrangell, 1839a,b, pp. 121-122). Holmberg (1856-1863, vol. 1, p. 284) considers the "Aglegmjuten," as he calls them, to occupy all the coastal region between the mouth of the Kuskokwim and the Alaska Peninsula. It is likely, however, that much of his information was taken from Wrangell.

Tikhmenev seems to have been the last roughly contemporary writer to deal with the subject. He mentions the "Alegmiut" and it is clear that he is referring to the people at the mouth of the Nushagak River since he makes no reference at all to upriver people (Tikhmenev, 1939-1940, pt. 2, p. 396). This basic distinction between coastal and interior peoples was followed in church records at Nushagak from 1842, when records were first kept, until the 1930's even though the population picture in the region became increasingly complicated throughout the nineteenth and well into the present century (Alaska Russian Church Archives, accession 12,766, vital statistics, Nushagak, 1842-1931).

After the purchase of Alaska by the United States, various authors attacked the problem of classifying the Eskimo enclaves of the territory. One of the earliest to do so was William H. Dall who, writing in 1870, appears to have been the first to use the term "Nushagagmiut" to refer to those people inhabiting the shores of Bristol Bay west of the Nushagak River to Cape Newenham, and up the river to the headwaters including the numerous lakes to the west. He equates this term with all the terms for the Nushagak River region used by Holmberg, Wrangell, and Tikhmenev (Dall, 1870, p. 405). Dall uses the term "Ogulmiut" to mean the inhabitants of the north shore of the Alaska Peninsula, north to the mouth of the Nushagak River and inland in an easterly direction to include the southern end of Iliamna Lake. On his map, the Nushagak River definitely represents the boundary between the Ogulmiut and the Nushagagmiut. The territory of the latter is shown as extending inland as far as the Nuyakuk River and includes the Togiak and its headwaters. Dall published a number of other classifications but they do not differ in any marked degree from this one.

Later authors have combined the classifications of Dall and the early Russians and some interesting variations can be noted. For example, Petroff (1884, map 2) equates the Nushagagmiut and the Kiatagmiut, and places the "Aglemute" on the north coast of the Alaska Peninsula, while Bancroft, 1886, vol. 1, p. 40) presents a classification that is essentially the same as Vasiliev's. Schanz (in Porter, 1893, p. 93) follows Dall with reference to the Nushagagmiut but places the Kiatagmiut in the southern Iliamna Lake region and on the Newhalen and Kvichak rivers. He also mentions the Aglemute as being in the Nushagak District but they are not specifically located. Hodge (1912, vol. 1, pp. 24, 682; vol. 2, p. 99) lists the Nushagagmiut as inhabiting the banks of the Igushik, Wood, and Nushagak rivers and the shores of Nushagak Bay, while the "Aglemiut" live along the coast from the mouth of the Nushagak River southwest to the valley of the Ugashik and extend eastward inland to the highlands. The Kiatagmiut in Hodge's classification are a subdivision of the Aglemiut inhabiting the banks of the Kvichak River and the shores of Iliamna Lake. Swanton (1952), in the most recent attempt to classify the Eskimo groupings in southwestern Alaska, seems to have followed Hodge almost completely.

Reliable population estimates for the Nushagak River region

during the period of early historic contact are difficult to arrive at because most sources tend to be extremely vague about the size and extent of the areas referred to. Nevertheless some reasonably reliable figures do exist and the emphasis here is on those estimates that appear to refer to the region under discussion.

The earliest explicit estimate of population in the Nushagak River region was made by Wrangell in 1825 (quoted in Petroff, 1884, p. 34). He lists the population of "Nushagak, Bristol Bay" as being 671. This presumably refers to the Eskimos living in the vicinity of the redoubt. Vasiliev in 1829 (reported by Zagoskin, 1956, p. 301) listed the Aglegmiut as consisting of 60 families with a total population of 500, while the Kiatagmiut numbered 400. Zagoskin himself believed these figures to be much too high and estimates that at the time of his explorations in southwestern Alaska thirteen years later, both tribes together numbered not more than 400 individuals. Unless Vasiliev's estimate is in error, the discrepancy may indicate the mortality caused by the smallpox epidemic of 1838-1839. Other contemporary sources, including Wrangell (1839a, p. 70; 1839b, pp. 121-122; Russian-American Company Records: Communications Sent, vol. 9, no. 460, folio 349) and Veniaminov (Barsukov, 1887-1888, vol. 2, p. 42) seem to follow Vasiliev and these are reasonable population estimates.

In 1886 Charles Bryant, a special agent of the Treasury Department, visited Nushagak and estimated that some 2,500 people inhabited the region within a forty mile radius of the settlement. This number seems excessively large, and it is possible that Bryant's figures are either simply wrong, or had been unduly influenced by seasonal migrants to the area (Bryant and McIntyre, 1869, p. 23). A more reasonable estimate for the period around 1860 is Tikhmenev's statement that 1,260 Eskimos lived in the vicinity of the Nushagak post. Even this number suggests that the aboriginal population was being rapidly supplemented by peoples moving in from other areas of southwestern Alaska (Tikhmenev, 1939-1940, pt. 2, p. 396). Slightly later Dall lists a population of 400 for the Nushagagmiut and he states explicitly that this figure refers only to those people living along the Nushagak River (Dall, 1875, p. 203; 1877, p. 19). However, he does not give a source for his figures and he may simply be repeating Vasiliev's estimate for the Kiatagmiut.

Population estimates in excess of 4,000 for the Bristol Bay area made in 1878 by V. Shishkin of the Nushagak mission (DRHA, vol. 1, p. 329) and repeated in 1880 by Ivan Petroff (1884, p. 72) appear to be greatly overstated, perhaps again owing to the double or even triple counting of seasonal migrants in the area. Petroff's Bristol Bay census district, however, included the coast of Bering Sea between Krenitzin Strait and Cape Newenham as well as the Ugashik, Naknek, Kvichak, Nushagak, Igushik, and Togiak rivers, but even so his figures seem high. Ten years later, Schanz, enumerating for the Eleventh Federal Census, and using Dall's definition of the Nushagagmiut, listed 170 people as belonging to that group (Porter, 1893, p. 158). Since his information was collected during the winter months, when some of the upriver people were resident in their interior villages rather than congregated in the Bay area, his enumeration could be reasonably correct. However, many families were doubtless away from the villages hunting and trapping. Assuming that Zagoskin's estimates are more accurate than Vasiliev's, there is reason to believe that the river population may have been this low in the 1890's. The estimate, nevertheless, seems rather too low.

More realistic population statistics, based on official Orthodox church sources, were made in 1895-1896, 1898, and 1899. In 1895-1896 there were said to be 358 Aglegmiut and 384 Kiatagmiut, while in 1898 the figures were 320 and 398 respectively (DRHA, vol. 5, pp. 11-13; Elliott, 1900, p. 740). A vital statistics record for the Nushagak mission in 1899 lists a total of 2,968 people within the influence of the mission; and the records explicitly exclude the Kuskokwim River from this count as well as any area that might be within the sphere of influence of the Kenai mission located at the site of the old Nikolaevski Redoubt on Cook Inlet (DRHA, vol. 2, p. 327). This number seems excessive even though we are told that in 1898 there were 1,566 "native Kuskaquim" people living "in or near Nushagak" (Elliott, 1900, p. 740). Many of these were almost certainly seasonal migrants to the bay area.

The final estimate to be discussed here was made by Moravian missionaries at the Carmel mission station in 1905. They acknowledged that their influence extended eighty miles up the river including an Eskimo population of 520, while there were another 400 people beyond this point (Hamilton, 1906, p. 31). This figure would appear to include the 100 people living at Kanulik, the Eskimo village near the Carmel mission, and possibly other bay settlements. Again these figures may not be excessive considering the number of people from other areas who appear to have been moving continually into the Nushagak River region during the nineteenth and early twentieth centuries. This Moravian estimate, together with the various Orthodox Church figures for the last decade of the nineteenth century, seem to be the most reliable of any of the census data. The figures are not only reasonably consistent with those of explorers early in the century, but they are made on the basis of subcultural divisions that have some meaning to informants at the present time.

During the summer of 1964, I conducted an archaeological survey of Nushagak Bay and the Nushagak River and its tributaries for the express purpose of locating settlements occupied during the nineteenth and early twentieth centuries. Forty-six sites were visited and mapped and, whenever possible, information concerning the sites and their period of occupancy was obtained from Eskimo informants living along the river. In many cases the names, size, and approximate locations of the sites had been extracted from historical source material prior to the field work. The information collected eventually will be incorporated into a detailed and documented study of settlement patterns in the Nushagak River region. Here I will simply summarize the data indicating the number and names of the settlements and derived population estimates for the period between 1800 and 1910. Where it has been impossible to determine village size directly from references in historical sources, estimates have been made based on an examination of the sites and on population statistics in the tenth and eleventh federal censuses (Petroff, 1884; Porter, 1893).

The Tikchik, Nuyakuk, and Nushagak rivers will be discussed first. Between 1800 and 1860 there were, for certain, only four occupied sites in the area, with the possibility of a fifth. Tikchik was located at the mouth of the river of that name, Agivavik south of the present community of New Stuyahok, and Akulivikchuk and Kokwok, also in the middle river area. The lower river is something of a mystery at this time, but there is a single small site, the name of which is not known, approximately twenty five miles from the mouth of the Wood River. Based on our information from these sites the total population of the region between these dates probably was somewhere between 400 and 500, a figure corresponding roughly to the data obtained by Vasiliev in 1829 (quoted in Zagoskin, 1956, p. 301).

Between 1860 and 1900 a number of new settlements came into existence to replace, in degree of importance, earlier ones. However, the basic continuity of upriver and middle river population centers was not greatly altered. Old Koliganek replaced Tikchik as the major upriver settlement; and in the middle river, three new villages appeared; Akokpak, Elilakok, and Tunravik. Probably no more than 100 persons ever occupied these three settlements. In the Kokwok-Akulivikchuk area we can discern a considerable shift in population. Agivavik and Akulivikchuk were abandoned and Kokwok was in a decided decline. Ekwok emerged as the major settlement for this section of the middle river and it has maintained this position down to the present time. The lower river still remained something of an enigma and although several small settlements were occupied, there were probably not, during this period, more than 75 people living between Ekwok and the mouth of the river. A conservative population estimate between 1860 and 1890 for the entire region would be approximately 400 people. This figure corresponds closely to the previously cited population statistics based on Orthodox church sources at the close of the century.

Turning to Nushagak Bay, we have noted that at the time of earliest contact there were four large and important settlements in the area, three on the east side and one on the west side of the bay. Ekuk, Kanakanak, Nushagak, and Kanulik, together with Igushik at the mouth of the Snake River must have contained all or most of the population of the bay when the Russians first appeared and for some time thereafter. It is probable that all five settlements began to grow after Alexandrovski Redoubt was established and Nushagak undoubtedly attracted the greatest number of new inhabitants. These people came from the interior area of the Nushagak River region, from the Kuskokwim River and other coastal and interior points in between, and from the Alaska Peninsula. By 1860 Tikhmenev's previously cited estimate of a population of 1,260 Eskimos in the bay area may not have been excessive, allowing for the probable inclusion of seasonal migrants.

The establishment of the salmon canning industry in Nushagak Bay in 1884, of course, had a profound effect upon the population and settlement pattern, an effect, at least as far as population was concerned, that was undoubtedly counterbalanced by periodic epidemics that swept the area. Just prior to 1884, on the basis of statistics in Petroff (1884), we can estimate the permanent population of the bay area at approximately 600 to 700 persons or perhaps slightly more. Kanulik, of course, was strongly affected by the establishment of a cannery in its vicinity in 1884 and the Moravian church two years later. Nushagak, Ekuk, and Aleknagik (Wood River Village) all received canneries around the turn of the century and the population of Kanakanak was certainly affected by economic development in its vicinity. Between 1870 and 1885 three small settlements sprang up north of Kanulik and it is certain that one of these, and perhaps all three, arose in response to the commercial fishery. About 1890, two new communities on the west side of the bay, New Kanakanak-Bradford and Chogiung, later called Dillingham, and other small settlements on both the east and west sides were established around 1910 or just after. The years 1908-1910 can perhaps be called a high point of the fishing industry in this area. There was approximately ten canneries in Nushagak Bay at that time and it is likely that the permanent Eskimo population of the area was from 700 to 800 people, a number that was augumented during the summer months by imported Oriental laborers, Eskimos from all over southwestern Alaska, and perhaps some Indians from the Iliamna Lake area. By 1920, after the influenza epidemic of 1918-1919, it is virtually certain that the permanent population of the bay did not exceed 500 persons.

Athabascans have occupied the Mulchatna River until fairly recent times and there is some indication that the lower section of the river was unoccupied during the early part of the historic period. The total period of Eskimo occupancy of the river in historic times appears to fall between 1890 and 1940, the period during which the settlement of Old Stuyahok was inhabited. It is tempting to suggest that the early inhabitants of this site were the first Eskimos on the river, but there are two small sites further up the river, the names of which are unknown, that may have been occupied briefly early in the twentieth century. The village of Kananakpok, a sizable settlement, belongs to the final fifteen or twenty years of Eskimo occupancy along the Mulchatna.

Old Stuyahok appears to have grown slowly and it would seem that the largest population on the Mulchatna occurred between 1920 and perhaps 1935 at a time when Kananakpok was also occupied. A reasonable estimate would place the number of inhabitants at that time between 90 and 125. In the late nineteenth and early twentieth centuries it is doubtful that the population ever exceeded 50 to 75. The lower river was abandoned around 1940 when the remaining inhabitants of the area moved onto the Nushagak River.

Reconstructing the settlement pattern along the Wood River is complicated by the fact that there are fewer references to these settlements in the sources than to those of any other part of the Nushagak River region. Of ten sites observed during the summer of 1964, only three can be dated with any degree of certainty and there are reliable population estimates for only two. Nevertheless, it is possible to make a few general statements. To begin with, there was no sizable population along the river until the period between 1850 and 1880. At that time Aleknagik (Wood River Village), Vuktuli, Imiak, and perhaps one other were inhabited and we can estimate a population for the river of perhaps 200 but probably not much more. Wood River village began to grow after a cannery was constructed there in 1901 and it may have included as many as 100 residents, even in winter, throughout the first decade and most of the second decade of this century. In fact, this period may have witnessed the heaviest population of the Wood River as a whole during the historic period.

The Wood River appears to have been extremely hard hit by the influenza epidemic of 1918-1919. The Eskimo population of the river was virtually wiped out and people did not begin to move back into the area until the late 1920's at which time families from the Togiak region, the Kuskokwim River, and Nushagak Bay began to populate the shores of Lake Aleknagik. Except for two families living at Wood River Village, the Wood River is today uninhabited.

We now turn to a closer examination of the problem of population movements into the Nushagak River region. The earliest
sources mention relations between the peoples of the area and
those from other parts of southwestern Alaska, particularly the
Kuskokwim River. In fact, John H. Kilbuck, the pioneer Moravian missionary on the Kuskokwim, claimed that the Eskimos of
that river often spoke to him of a "warrior people" who once lived
along the river and a remnant of which, in the 1880's, resided on
Nunivak Island and in a village or two at the mouth of the Nushagak River. At one time, according to Kilbuck's informants, these
people occupied the lower Kuskokwim River and Nelson Island,
and they harassed the other Kuskokwim Eskimos. Eventually
these "warrior people" were defeated and withdrew to the Nushagak and to Nunivak Island. After this the Kuskokwim Eskimos
made frequent trips to the mouth of the Nushagak to fight the
"warrior people." The Russians put a stop to the fighting. The
Kuskokwim people told Kilbuck that the village of Ekuk on the
east shore of Nushagak Bay was populated by "warrior people"
(Kilbuck Papers, box 7, folder 1, no. 6).

Whatever may be the elements of truth in this legend, the earliest Russian sources make clear that militant hostility existed between the Kuskokwim Eskimos and those of Nushagak Bay.
Berkh mentions that the chief success of the Korsakovski expedition was that the peoples of the Kuskokwim and the Glakmiut
(Aglegmiut) were reconciled (Berkh, 1823, p. 47). Khromchenko
a few years later in 1822 makes no reference to the Kuskokwim
Eskimos but maintains that Fedor Kolmakov had, almost single-
handedly, made peace between the Aglegmiut and the Kiatagmiut. The Aglegmiut are described by Khromchenko as having been
the most barbarous people along the Alaska coast between Bristol
Bay and Norton Sound. However, warfare had greatly reduced
their numbers, and they had found it necessary to take refuge
with Kolmakov who presumably was successful in maintaining at
least enough peace so that the fur trade could be carried on with
both groups (Khromchenko, 1824, pt. 11, pp. 39-41). Early reports
of general managers of the Russian-American Company also mention how the Aglegmiut, apparently displaced from Nunivak Island, sought protection from their enemies through friendship

with the Russians at Alexandrovski Redoubt (Russian-American Company Records: Communications Sent, vol. 9, no. 460, folio 349). Warfare had scattered them, but with Kolmakov's assistance, they grouped themselves in villages near the redoubt (Russian-American Company Records: Communications Sent, vol. 3, no. 164, folio 270). Zagoskin believed that the Aglegmiut and the Kiatagmiut were merely Kuskokwim people who migrated southward in the late prehistoric period to occupy the shores of Bristol Bay and the banks of the Nushagak River. The Aglegmiut thus stand identified as the "warrior people" of Kilbuck's Kuskokwim informants and it is likely that they fought not only with their immediate neighbors but with other peoples who came into the Nushagak Bay area.

Although the mixture of population in this area undoubtedly precedes the period of historic contact, we also know that the new Alexandrovski Redoubt attracted peoples from both the north and south (DRHA, vol. 4, pp. 243-244). In 1829 Veniaminov wrote that not only Aglegmiut, but also people from the Kuskokwim and various points on the Alaska Peninsula, could be seen at the redoubt (Barsukov, 1897-1901, vol. 1, p. 14). We have noted previously that in the winter of 1829-1830, 200 Kuskokwim men came, at Kolmakov's invitation, to Lake Aleknagik to trade (Russian-American Company Records: Communications Sent, vol. 7, no. 257, folio 272). In the summer of 1868 White refers to a party of Tanaina Indians who had come to Nushagak from Cook Inlet by way of Iliamna Lake and the Kvichak River (White, 1869, p. 6). Apparently Aleuts occasionally visited the redoubt and in 1878, some of these along with Kuskokwim Eskimos and Tanaina were living in the area under the jurisdiction of the Nushagak mission (DRHA, vol. 2, p. 330). Representatives of the same subcultural groups are also mentioned in 1879 and 1883 and although Kiatagmiut continued to be the most numerous group along the Nushagak River, Eskimos from the Kuskokwim already greatly outnumbered Aglegmiut in the bay region (DRHA, vol. 2, pp. 146-147; Bailey, 1880, pp. 26-27; Elliott, 1900, p. 740). Ivan Petroff, in collecting data for the Tenth Census, noted that families from the Kuskokwim, Yukon Delta, and Norton Sound were living in the vicinity of Nushagak. Many of these people were engaged in hunting walrus along the shallow coast (Petroff, 1884, p. 136).

People living on the Nushagak River today represent many different subcultural enclaves, and many of them know legends that tell of the time their ancestors came from the Kuskokwim River and other areas. Upriver people consider those who live permanently on the coast to be a "little different" but they are not precise about what these differences are. One informant, born at Igushik at the mouth of the Snake River, had been sent up to Kanakanak (Bradford) to attend school and to live with her aunt who had been born and raised at Chogiung. This was in the late 1920's, and was the first time the girl had had an opportunity to meet people from Ekwok and other Nushagak River points. She and her aunt always thought that these people were different from the people from the bay area. She could understand their dialect but they seemed to talk faster and were in other ways "a little different." This girl recognized the term Kiatagmiut and confirmed that it meant upriver people. Other informants on the Kvichak River recognized the term Aglegmiut and indicated that this group occupied the area from the mouth of the Nushagak through the Kvichak and Alagnak rivers east to Kukaklek and Nonvianuk lakes (personal communication from Joan B. Townsend).

The great influenza epidemic of 1918-1919, which appears to have been more severe in this area than in almost any other part of Alaska, was an important factor in the more recent population shifts in the Nushagak River region. An orphanage was established at Kanakanak in the latter year to care for the many children orphaned by the epidemic. Many young men and women, after leaving the orphange, preferred either to stay in the bay area or move up the Nushagak River rather than return to their original homes. A resident of Ekwok in 1964 illustrates this situation clearly. Born at Ugashik on the Alaska Peninsula, he was brought to the orphanage after the death of his parents in 1918. He moved up the river to Ekwok in the early 1920's as a young man and has lived there ever since.

This overview on population groupings at the time of contact can be summed up by emphasizing three points already made.

First of all, most of the early sources make a distinction between coastal and inland populations in the area. It seems logical to accept the Khromchenko-Vasiliev distinction between the Kiatagmiut and Aglegmiut since these terms have at least some meaning to informants at the present time and since the Nushagak area populations were closest to the aboriginal pattern of distribution at the time they were observed by these explorers. Secondly, there was a mixed population in the Nushagak River region even at the time of earliest contact, and the duality of the Kiat and Aglegmiut was already in a state of flux before the Russians appeared on the scene. Thirdly, this trend began, in all probability, in the prehistoric period, continued through the nineteenth century, with movements from the Kuskokwim being particularly common, and was accentuated during the early twentieth century by epidemics that further obliterated the aboriginal distinction between coastal and inland peoples. As a result of all these trends, little can be observed of the aboriginal population groupings and these can be only partially reconstructed through the use of the historic source material together with the vague and uncertain information that can be collected from present inhabitants of the area.

VIII

The Yearly Cycle
in the Nineteenth Century

❖◆

WE NOW TURN TO A CONSIDERATION OF THE SEASONAL CYCLE OF SUB-
sistence activities followed by the Eskimos of the Nushagak River
region during the early period of historic contact. Much of the
material presented here has been taken from historical sources
which, in many cases, are neither sufficiently detailed nor explicit. Of necessity, most of this information applies to the period
between 1880 and 1910, and the picture of seasonal activities that
is sketched is, in many ways, certain to differ considerably from
the one that prevailed during the late prehistoric period. Where
possible, these data have been supplemented by information collected from elderly informants during field work in the summers
of 1964 and 1965.

Fall. When the first snow fell in early October, the Nushagak
River Eskimo men returned to their permanent villages along the
river from their hunting and trapping camps in the interior. They
traveled down the tributaries of the Nushagak or perhaps along
the coast and into the bay in the case of people living in that
area. The people of the bay and lower river used the characteristic skin-covered kayak, while further up the river birchbark ca-
noes were presumably used during much of the period under
consideration. Petroff noted that the Nushagak Eskimos he saw in
1890 were using a "clumsy contrivance," a heavy frame of birch
poles covered with caribou skins to which hair still adhered

(Petroff, 1891, p. 2). Such a craft might be constructed by an interior hunting and trapping party for the specific purpose of transporting people, game, traps, and other gear back to the permanent villages along the river (Oswalt, 1963, p. 126). By the middle of October most people would be settled for the winter and occupied with repairs to houses and caches. In early fall some trapping seems to have been done near the villages. Deadfall traps are mentioned as having been set for marten at this time (Elliott, 1886, p. 381). When ice formed on the river about the end of October or early in November, traps for whitefish were placed under it and grayling were taken with hooks through holes in the ice.

How much hunting was done during this period is not certain, but it is likely that caribou were hunted near the villages and perhaps for some distance up the river. Elderly informants at Dillingham reported that inhabitants of the bay region near the turn of the century made lengthy fall hunting trips up the river and into the Mulchatna country for caribou, but this is not mentioned in any of the sources. These same coastal peoples could take ling cod and blackfish through the ice not far from their villages. Also in November families from Chogiung and other bay communities would travel up the Wood River to Lake Aleknagik in order to fish for trout through the ice with hooks. Frozen trout, stacked like cordwood, were brought back to the villages by dog team.

Winter. It is probable that, during the aboriginal period, most fall activities in both river and coastal communities ended in early December when the severe winter weather settled in for good. By that time the inhabitants had repaired their houses and made themselves as comfortable as possible. At this time of year the permanent river villages were fully occupied and all mobility had ceased. (After historic contact, however, there appears to have been greater mobility during the winter months.) Fall trapping continued throughout the winter and, according to informants, steel traps were uncommon and most of the foxes and beaver were trapped with snares and deadfalls. Zagoskin mentions that at the time of his explorations in the Yukon and Kuskokwim valleys in 1842-1844, the natives would not change their traditional methods of trapping. When acquiring steel traps, they immediately converted the various parts into knives, axes, rings, and other useful implements (Zagoskin, 1956, p. 222).

An elderly man at New Koliganek said that the inhabitants of Tikchik near the mouth of the Tikchik River trapped further up the river during the winter and hunted caribou along the Nuyakuk River and north of it on the vast tundra between the Tikchik and Nushagak rivers. Caribou were plentiful at that time, according to the informant, but moose were very scarce. The Tikchik hunters and trappers apparently left their families in the village and seldom ranged more than a two days' journey from home.

It is perhaps worthwhile to describe in some detail the houses of the Nushagak River region. Petroff's description of the dwellings he encountered in the area while enumerating for the Tenth Federal Census is the most detailed of any nineteenth-century observer. It may be assumed that this house form is very close to that constructed by the people during the aboriginal period.

> The houses in all this district outside of the missionary settlement of Nushagak are much the same as in the other northern divisions, and may be described as follows: A circular mound of earth, grass-grown and littered with all sorts of household utensils, a small spiral coil of smoke rising from the apex, dogs crouching upon it, children climbing or rolling down, stray morsels of food left from one meal to the other, and a soft mixture of mud and offal surrounding it all. The entrance to this house is a low, irregular, square aperture, through which the inmate stoops and passes down a foot or two through a short, low passage onto the earthen floor within. The interior generally consists of an irregularly-shaped square or circle twelve or fifteen or twenty feet in diameter, receiving its only light from without through the small smoke-opening at the apex of the roof, which rises, tentlike, from the floor. The fireplace is directly under this opening. Rude beds or couches of skins and grass mats are laid, slightly raised above the floor, upon clumsy frames made of sticks and saplings or rough-hewn planks, and sometimes on little elevations built up of peat or sod. Sometimes a small hallway with bulging sides is erected over the entrance, where by this expansion room is afforded for the keeping of utinsils [sic] and water-vessels and as a shelter for dogs.
>
> In the interior regions, where both fuel and building material are more abundant, the houses change somewhat in appearance and construction; the excavation of the coast houses, made for the purpose of saving both articles just mentioned, disappears and gives way to log structures above the ground, but still covered

with sod. Living within convenient distance of timber, the people here do not depend so much upon the natural warmth of mother earth (Petroff, 1884, p. 15).

Nineteenth-century houses excavated at Tikchik during the summer of 1965 were almost identical to the first type described above.

Both Petroff (1891, p. 2) and, approximately ten years later, the enumerator of the Eleventh Federal Census emphasize the poor construction of houses in the Nushagak River region, the latter going so far as to consider them "among the most wretched habitations to be found in Alaska" (Porter, 1893, p. 170). They were carelessly constructed, probably because of their seasonal occupancy, and the roofs reportedly fell in each year with the melting snow of spring.

The major winter activities in the villages of the Nushagak River region were the dances and dance festivals that began in late December or early January and lasted until February. The winter ceremonies of this area were never described in detail by contemporary observers. Some of the ceremonies appear to have been purely secular while others doubtless had supernatural implications and seem to have centered about the propitiation of the dead and possibly the magical revival of game animals. The center of these winter festivities was the *kashgee,* or ceremonial house, at least one of which was to be found in all the larger settlements. These structures were similar in construction to the dwellings, but much larger. The *kashgee* at Kokwok, for example, was noted throughout the area for its huge side planks which were as much as five inches thick, three feet broad, and up to fifty feet in length (Schanz, 1891, no. 1881, pp. 138-139). Residents of other settlements would be invited for many of the festivals, and the singing and dancing in the *kashgee* frequently continue for ten days or more (Porter, 1893, pp. 93-94).

The only detailed description of a Nushagak area *kashgee* is given by Governor A. P. Swineford who presumably saw the one at Nushagak during his tour of Alaska in 1888. He not only describes the structure, but briefly discusses the activities which took place within it.

To enter . . . you first climb down into a hole in the ground five or six feet, then crawl 10 or 15 feet through a low tunnel to where

you ascend to a level with the roof of the tunnel and find yourself
in a large room. . . . A raised platform extends all around the four
sides leaving room in the center for the fireplace, which is simply
a bare, square spot of earth some three feet below the surrounding platform upon which an open fire can be built. The platform
is on a level with the top of the entrance tunnel, the end of which
can be opened at will so as to permit persons to pass under the
platform to the fireplace. . . . When the fireplace is not needed, it
is covered over with planks even with the platform, so that there
is no break in the floor. In this house the men do all their domestic
work such as construction of bidarkis, the manufacture of sleds,
etc., and in it all public meetings or councils are held and all public
business transacted. It is also open at all times as a shelter for
guests or visitors, who are there entertained instead of being taken
to this or that private habitation. It is the sleeping place for un-
married adult males, and it is likewise used as a bath house. . . .
The *kashima* also answers the purpose of a theatre, for mask
dancers and representations. Both males and females take part in
scenic performances, in which there are combats between men
who shed bladderfuls of seal blood for effect, where stuffed animals are moved about by hidden strings, devils masks with move-
able eyes introduced, and wooden birds made to flap their wings.
In these representations the actors enter through the fire hole,
like those who bob up through a trap door in the stage of one of
our theatres (Swineford, 1898, pp. 164-166).

It is doubtful whether Governor Swineford, during his brief
summer visit to Nushagak, ever witnessed any of the ceremonies
he so graphically describes, but his picture of the *kashgee* and its
associated activities is doubtless an accurate portrayal, in a general way, of this hub of village winter work, play, and ceremonies. The *kashgee* to which he refers closely resembles one excavated at Tikchik during the summer of 1965.

The dances and festival in the *kashgee*, then, were the high
point of the winter and they were held in this region, as in other
parts of Alaska, at a time when ordinary subsistence activities
were, of necessity, greatly restricted. As Nelson has pointed out
for the Yukon and Kuskokwim regions to the north, these festivals may have served mainly to help pass the long, dark winter
days (Nelson, 1899, p. 357). It is also true, however, that they
served to promote friendly relations between neighboring villages
and, perhaps most important of all, they were essential as an
expression of the religious beliefs of the people (see Oswalt, 1963,
chap. 3).

Spring. In late February or early March many Nushagak River families prepared to move from their permanent communities on the riverbank to temporary camps along streams in the mountainous country of the interior. Boats and all household equipment were moved by dog sled and apparently some families did not leave their villages until April. The main occupation at this time of the year was the taking of fur-bearing animals. The most valuable pelts, at least toward the end of the Russian period, were beaver, otter, red fox, bear, arctic fox, marten, lynx, mink, muskrat, and wolf (Russian-American Company Records: Communications Sent, vol. 38, no. 115, folio 29). Beaver were taken mainly by digging them out of their houses (DRHA, vol. 1, p. 329; Elliott, 1886, pp. 381-384), although the Russian-American Company officially disapproved of this method because of long-range harmful effects on the beaver population (Russian-American Company Records: Communications Sent, vol. 16, no. 467, folio 178). Caribou were also hunted extensively at this time of the year, probably mainly with rifles or old flintlock muskets by 1880 (DRHA, vol. 1, p. 329), although Petroff insists that as late as 1890, Eskimos with firearms were infrequently encountered in the area (1891, p. 6).

While the river Eskimos were in the interior hunting caribou and trapping fur-bearing animals, coastal residents of Nushagak Bay, in addition to interior trapping, hunted seals in the Point Protection or Igushik areas. Toward the close of the nineteenth century, at least, most of the hunting was done with rifles from shore. Dip netting for smelt was also a late spring activity for coastal families. Some individuals stated that occasionally river Eskimos would come down to the coast in the late spring to hunt seals and then would stay on to fish, perhaps selling a few fresh fish to canneries in order to obtain money to buy food and other supplies before returning upriver.

Summer. By the middle of June most river families were concentrated in their winter villages to prepare for salmon fishing. This meant repairing their traps, constructed of split spruce strips, so that they could be used effectively when the fish began to run. The mouth of the Nushagak River was a favorite spot for fishing with traps, while at the rapids on the upper Nuyakuk salmon were taken with spears and dip nets (Elliott, 1886, pp. 381-384; Cobb, 1907, p. 32; Bower, 1926, pp. 108-110). Although some Nushagak River families stayed on the river to fish during June and July, many more migrated to the coast to fish and visit the trading post. This was probably increasingly true after commercial fishing was introduced. However, even prior to this time, the pattern seems to have been for the river Eskimos to visit the Nushagak post in early summer with their furs and then either remain to put up fish or return up the river. The above-mentioned New Koliganek man, speaking of the period just before 1900, said that in early summer not long after the river ice broke up, the residents of Tikchik would go down to the Nushagak post to trade their furs. They traveled down the Nushagak River in large boats covered with caribou skins or brown bear hides that were similar to the type already described. The trappers would trade their furs at the post and receive tea, flour, sugar, tobacco, gun powder, crackers, etc. in exchange. Trade was also carried on with coastal peoples, with products of the interior being exchanged for seal oil and other coastal products. The Tikchik people apparently did not stay long on the coast but returned to their village in order to be on hand to catch and dry salmon. When the time came for the return trip, the large boats were abandoned or traded for small sealskin-covered kayaks and the villagers, often traveling as a group, returned to Tikchik by way of the Wood River and the lakes. This was considered to be much easier than paddling up the Nushagak and Nuyakuk rivers, since there was only the one extensive portage from the Wood River Lakes system to the Tikchik Lakes.

Fish caught by Nushagak area residents were dried on racks. The heads were sometimes buried in the ground and allowed to rot slightly before being eaten. Fish eggs were put up in seal oil and considered a delicacy to be eaten during the winter festivals (Elliott, 1886, pp. 381-384; SPG Proceedings, 1888, pub. 1888, p. 29). As previously mentioned, there always seems to have been work for some Eskimos at the canneries, usually on a day-to-day basis.

Walrus hunting was an important activity in Nushagak Bay and surrounding area during the Russian period. Between 1827

and 1830, 452 *puds*[1] of walrus tusks were shipped from Alexandrovski Redoubt and in 1838 alone nearly 200 *puds* (Russian-
American Company Records: Communications Sent, vol. 12, no.
256, folio 152; vol. 16, no. 479, folio 189). By 1890, however, most
of the animals had disappeared. Reference has already been
made to the fact that the Eskimos of the area, presumably the
Aglegmiut, were skilled ivory carvers. They carved paper cutters,
salad forks, salt spoons, watch chains, and other objects for sale to
the post and to white cannery workers (Swineford, 1898, pp.
162-163). Beluga were hunted along the shores of Nushagak Bay
throughout the summer months, and moulting birds would also
be taken and eggs gathered to put up in seal oil.

By the last week in July the great runs of salmon had passed
and, except on the upper river, fishing ended. In mid-August
many men ascended the tributaries of the Nushagak for the interior, leaving the women and children in the villages to watch over
the full fish caches. Caribou hunting was good at this time of the
year and many skins were secured for winter clothing. During the
Russian period fall caribou skins were taken in trade at the Nushagak post for shipment to Sitka from where they were distributed
to posts in areas where caribou were not plentiful (Russian-American Company Records: Communications Sent, vol. 9, no. 318,
folio 478). In mid-September the fur of the beaver would again
be in prime condition and these animals were taken in wooden
deadfalls or their dams were broken and the water allowed to run
out, exposing the beaver. This hunting and trapping continued
until the first snow fall in October when the men returned once
again to their winter villages (DRHA, vol. 1, p. 329; Elliott, 1886,
pp. 381-384; Osgood, 1904, p. 18).

The seasonal cycle described above is roughly the same for
both the river Eskimos and those living on the shores of Nushagak Bay. Only in the spring did any major difference occur, when
the coastal people did most of their sea mammal hunting. The
distinction between the coastal and interior way of life was very
likely greater in the aboriginal period before both groups of people were drawn into the fur trade. Nevertheless, the Aglegmiut
were never primarily sea mammal hunters but emphasized fishing

---

[1] One *pud* equals approximately thirty-six pounds.

and were always more inland-oriented than many coastal Eskimos to the north.

By the turn of the century, Eskimos of the Nushagak River region already exhibited many of the outward manifestations of acculturation to a marked degree. In the villages around Nushagak Bay, the traditional houses had been modified with windows and hinged doors, while interior furnishings included such items as iron stoves, kettles, and dishes. Aboriginal clothing, at least during the summer, had been almost entirely replaced by "store clothes" purchased from the trader. The rapid growth of the salmon canning industry certainly speeded up the acculturation process in this area. The familiarity of the Eskimos with home-brewing processes has already been mentioned and the enumerator of the Eleventh Federal Census noted that the trader at Nushagak, attempting to limit the making of home-brewed beverages, limited the amounts of sugar and flour that a customer could purchase. The Eskimos, however, "have frequently been discovered saving up this flour and sugar, depriving themselves of sweetening for their tea and not eating bread until they have enough for a brew" (Porter, 1893, p. 94). The Nushagak people were said to indulge extensively in cigarette smoking and card playing, and to hold in considerable scorn those Eskimos of the Togiak and Kuskokwim rivers who had less contact with whites (Spurr, 1900, pp. 89-90).

Throughout the nineteenth century and into the twentieth the Nushagak River Eskimos were in fairly frequent contact with the Tanaina Athabascans from the upper Mulchatna River, Iliamna Lake, and Cook Inlet. Parties of Indians occasionally visited the Nushagak post, and it is certain that further contacts would occur in the process of hunting and trapping expeditions into the interior (Petroff, 1884, pp. 135-136; 1891, p. 2).

IX

The Nushagak River Today

◆◇◆

WE NOW TURN OUR ATTENTION TO THE YEARLY CYCLE OF THE CON-
temporary Nushagak River Eskimos and the settlement pattern of
the region. (In this chapter, such phrases as "at present" and
"today" refer to the time of the field research—1964-1965.)

Fall. The Eskimos of the river villages of Ekwok, New Stuyahok, Koliganek, and Portage Creek usually return to their homes
around the middle of August after having spent the summer in
various locations on Nushagak Bay. The silver salmon are just beginning to run at this time and the run will continue for about
two weeks, after which the salmon fishing will be over for the
year. Families who did not put up fish during the summer will do
so at this time. A few red and humpbacked salmon may still be
working their way up the river in late August and a vigorous subsistence fishery is carried out in all the villages until the last sil-
vers have passed. At this time too, many men hunt ducks in the
sloughs near the villages where these birds flock preparatory to
heading south. While duck hunting the men may also look for
brown bears since these animals like to come to the river bank to
fish for spawned-out salmon.

The moose hunting season opens on the twentieth of August
and by that time many families have put up their fish for the winter. Many have completed their subsistence fishing at summer fish
camps on the bay and when the fishing boats come up the river in
late summer they are sometimes loaded with dried fish and also
with supplies for the winter that have been purchased with

money earned during the commercial fishing season. The salmon canneries frequently provide a grubstake to fishermen; this has either been taken out of their summer income or advanced against the next summer's earnings. In this way the canneries are able to bind a particular fisherman from year to year.

Most of the fall moose hunting takes place in the Mulchatna River region or along the Kokwok River where many moose have spent the summer near lakes to escape the mosquitos and flies. Some men leave their villages for these areas nearly as soon as they have deposited their families at home. However, a moose killed early in the season is difficult to preserve and since the season extends through the end of the year, winter trapping and hunting are frequently combined. The Nushagak River is not noted for an abundance of game animals. Moose hunting here is a relatively recent activity since the animals have moved into the general area only within the past twenty or twenty-five years. There are caribou in the Mulchatna and Nuyakuk river regions and these are also hunted in winter and fall. All informants, naturally enough, speak of their hunting activities strictly in terms of the legal seasons.

For late summer and fall travel on the Nushagak River and its tributaries, the large commercial fishing boats which the Eskimos own for their summer fishing on the bay are generally not used. A wide variety of skiffs seen around the villages reflect a tendency to copy the more sporting commercial models or actually to buy them through mail order catalogues or dealers in Dillingham. The typical Nushagak River skiff, however, is constructed in the village with hardwood obtained from a store. These boats are about fifteen feet in length and approximately three and one-half to four feet wide with flaring sides. The bow turns up slightly and there is a small amount of decking at the very front. The ribs are spaced about a foot apart and there may or may not be gunwales running around the sides. There are usually three seats including the one at the back. The stern piece is of double thickness with a deep, long notch to receive an outboard motor. As might be expected, these boats are very heavy. They are frequently repaired and sometimes taken completely apart, the soggy sections of wood replaced, and the whole vessel recaulked and repainted. During the summers of 1964 and 1965 no outboard motors of less than nine horsepower were observed in use on the river, and most men seemed to feel that a large, heavy skiff should be powered by at least a fifteen horsepower engine. There is a growing tendency, however, for the boats to get smaller and the motors larger; so that in the minds of many younger people, a "skiff and kicker" is just a plaything and not a useful piece of equipment.

Another type of river transportation was observed at New Koliganek in the form of long, narrow, open-decked kayaks, but residents stated that these were not used very much anymore. It was true that the four vessels of this type examined were in a very poor state of repair. These river kayaks are approximately twelve to thirteen feet in length, about two feet wide, and are pointed at both ends. They are made of thin strips of spruce, and the ribbing is lashed in place with ordinary light twine. The canvas cover is tacked on and then painted with a grey marine finish. Inside the boat is a slat seat lashed together with string. The occupant can either kneel or sit with his legs outstretched and when the small vessel is in the water, there appears to be no more than six or eight inches of freeboard amidships. These kayaks are propelled with a single-bladed paddle, the blade of which is long, narrow and ribbed on both sides. For propelling the boat in shallow water, two narrow poles about four feet in length are used, one on either side of the boat. Today these vessels are used primarily by middle-aged and older men for checking nets located close to the village.

The late summer and fall in a Nushagak River community is a time of considerable activity and preparation for the long winter months. Some men make repairs to their houses or make one or more trips to Dillingham in their fishing boats to pick up stove oil, lumber, or large food orders. Others pull their fishing boats out of the water for the winter. The care and maintenance of the fishing boats, the Eskimo's single most valuable and expensive possession on which he depends for mobility throughout much of the year and for most of his yearly income, takes a great deal of time and effort at all seasons.

On a typical early fall day at New Koliganek in 1965 people were observed at a variety of tasks that can be considered characteristic of village life near the end of the fishing season. Some women were cutting fish while their husbands and older sons

were stringing these on racks to dry in the sun. A man was hauling logs from upriver behind his skiff preparatory to building a
storm shed on the front of his new house. Another man was building an elevated cache from old lumber purchased in Dillingham
when a cannery was demolished. Two men related by marriage
were repairing the engine of the older man's fishing boat; changing the oil, cleaning the spark plugs, starting and restarting the
motor. A man and his two young sons were engaged in completely rebuilding an old skiff while several women washed clothes in
gasoline-powered washing machines and took advantage of the
sunny, warm weather to hang them up to dry.

Winter. The legal trapping season for most fur-bearing animals
in the Nushagak River region has, in recent years, opened on November 10. Some mink trapping takes place in the late fall and
early winter but only a few trappers are seriously interested in
this animal. Even those who do trap for mink do not pursue the
activity vigorously, but are usually content to set a few traps
close to the village. Several New Koliganek individuals stated
that mink trapping in the vicinity of that village amounted to
practically nothing; a trapper would be fortunate to take five or
six animals. Further up the river the trapping for all fur bearers is
better, but not many New Koliganek residents care to make the
trip. Trapping is also spoken of as being very good in the sloughs
and small lakes that characterize the lower river. A New Koliganek man seemed to think that there was no point in trapping at
all unless it was possible to earn at least $2,000 during the winter.
However, the prices paid for mink and other furs have dropped
and it is almost impossible to make this much. Another trapper
noted that about seven years ago he had what he considered to be
a "real good" trapping season when he took 30 mink, 10 otter, and
earned $1,100. The mink season ends on the thirty-first of January
and there is no limit to the number of animals that a trapper may
take.

Winter travel in the Nushagak River region is almost exclusively by dog team although at least two men, one at New Koliganek
and the other at New Stuyahok, have experimented with snow-
mobiles. Few men have more than five or six dogs and many use
only three. Sleds, made locally of spruce, are relatively large and
heavy. They are rectangular and do not curve up much at the

front; most do not have brakes. Plywood is sometimes used for the basket, and nails and wire are extensively employed in the sled's construction. Long metal sled shoes screwed to the runners are used during the spring. Dog harnesses are made entirely of webbing and have no snaps, only a metal ring at the back. The harnesses consist of two pieces of webbing that run along the dog's back, cross under his chest, and then come up along his side. All joints are sewn with heavy thread and no rivets are used. Dogs are hitched in pairs with either a single or double leader. A short line from the back of each harness leads to a long towline; another short line from the dog's collar to the towline helps to keep the animal in position.

Trappers often wear snowshoes, particularly when moving off the trails to check their traps. The type used is approximately three and one-half to four feet in length and tapers sharply at the rear; the front turns up only slightly. Snowshoes examined by the author were rather poorly made, particularly at the front where little or no care had been taken to bend the wood in such a way that it would not split. The *babiche* used is crudely made and split areas of the frame are frequently bound with string.

Winter is not a time of intensive subsistence activity. There is some caribou hunting, particularly by upriver residents of the village of New Koliganek. In the foothills of Ketok Mountain the caribou hunting is usually good and the villagers do have to go far to take them. In November and December moose are frequently hunted along the wooded tributaries of the Nushagak. There is fishing through the ice, particularly with hooks for grayling and pike. One New Koliganek informant said that some men set nets under the ice for whitefish [but the author's impression was that winter fishing of any kind is more talked about than actually done], but the people depend mostly on the dry fish they put up during the summer and early fall. Hares, ptarmigan, and other small game are frequently taken and much time is spent in hauling firewood. This midwinter period, then, is one of relative inactivity and it parallels that of the early contact period when the great festivals and dances in the *kashgee* were performed. Today church holidays during the winter and early spring, particularly Russian Christmas, are important events and much visiting takes place between villages at this time. Some men will make trips by air or dog team to Dillingham for supplies once or twice during the winter.

Spring. Following the midwinter lull, spring trapping begins. The beaver season opens on the first of February. Trappers are more energetic in their efforts to take this animal, particularly those Eskimos living at Ekwok who trap up Klutuk Creek or in the low country on the east side of the river. New Koliganek trappers trap along the Nushagak above the mouth of the Nuyakuk. The limit on beavers is 15 animals and it has been unusual in recent years for a trapper to receive more than $20.00 each for the blankets he takes. New Koliganek trappers are particularly discouraged about the chances of making good money by trapping beaver because of the low price paid even for prime pelts. Although all trappers are aware that pelts sent to buyers in Seattle and other southern locations bring a higher price, a relatively small amount of fur is exported directly from the villages. Most trappers take their furs to Dillingham in March at the time of the annual "Beaver Round Up" when fur buyers visit the town in order to purchase furs. In 1965 the "Round Up" was held from March 18 to 21, following the end of the short beaver trapping season. This is a time of celebration with dog races, dances, and other activities, as well as much drinking. The local airline and various independent pilots offer special rates from the villages to Dillingham at this time and many families make the trip.

In spite of the local emphasis on beaver trapping, the people of the Nushagak River region do not really rely heavily on income derived from trapping. At best, money obtained through the sale of furs is a valuable supplement to income earned during the summer months and carries many Nushagak families through a period of the year when there are few opportunities to obtain cash. Nor do the trappers devote a great deal of time and energy to the activity. New Stuyahok informants, when questioned concerning the amount of time spent on the trap lines, noted that it was unusual for a trapper to be away from the village for more than four or five days at a time. The men almost always want to be back in the village for the weekend, particularly for the showing of films on Friday nights. Therefore, their trap lines are always located near the village and they make no elaborate ar-

rangements for camping in the bush. One New Stuyahok informant said that when he was a small boy, his father had a trapping
cabin on the Kokwok River but that it had not been used for
many years. In recent years, he has trapped due west from the
village and more often than not he can visit his traps and return
the same day.

Beginning in mid April, ducks and geese arrive in the Nushagak River region and there is good hunting throughout the area,
particularly in the sloughs near the villages.

Summer. By late in May the four Nushagak River villages are
virtually abandoned as the men with their families move to Bristol Bay to take part in the commercial salmon fishing. King
salmon begin the run shortly after the first of June and most men
have their boats in the water well before this date. In recent years
Koliganek-New Koliganek families have camped along the beach
just north of Snag Point, while some Ekwok families camp less
than a mile north of Wood River Village. Since Ekwok and Portage Creek are the villages closest to Nushagak Bay, many families remain there all summer to put up dry fish. The men may pay
quick visits to the settlements during periods when the fishing is
closed. In the case of Portage Creek these visits are made by
boat, but at Ekwok several villagers may charter a small plane
and arrange for the pilot to return for them before the next
fishing period opens. Beginning in 1963, families from New Stuyahok established a fish camp at Lewis Point on the north bank of
the Nushagak about fifteen miles above its mouth. The subsistence fishery is thought to be better there than in the vicinity of
Dillingham and at the same time the men can easily visit their
families during the closed periods. The women have a good supply of dried salmon put up by the time the commercial fishing
season is over.

Although the importance and all-pervading influence of commercial fishing in the Nushagak River region tends to overshadow
the subsistence fishery, it is necessary not to underestimate the
importance of the latter in the economy of the river Eskimos. The
fish put up and dried in the summer fish camps along the bay or
during late summer and early fall in the river villages is of vital
importance as a winter food supply for both humans and dogs.
The subsistence catch of salmon for the Nushagak River, in-

cluding Nushagak Bay, in 1965 was officially listed by the Dillingham area office of the Alaska Department of Fish and Game as 135,900 fish and there is reason to believe that this figure is in error on the conservative side (Nelson and Siedelman, n.d.).

As previously noted, along the river the women prepare fish for drying after the men have checked and emptied the nets. At summer fish camps on the bay women handle every aspect of the subsistence fishery except the construction of drying racks. A fish prepared for drying is slit down the underside in such a way that the backbone is separated from both sides. If the fish are for human consumption, this backbone section is usually removed, but if they are intended for dog food, it may be left attached. The outside surfaces of the fish are sliced in order to facilitate drying. Fish racks are of relatively simple construction consisting of sturdy corner posts, connected at the top by slender horizontal poles between which a horizontal series of even lighter poles are hung. The fish, tails up, are draped over these poles. The racks often have a roof frame so that a canvas cover can be hung to protect the drying fish from rain. When the fish are first hung, flies lay eggs on them, but if there is even a slight breeze and the fish are drying properly, the maggots drop off soon after they hatch. If the fish are intended for dog food, no particular care is taken to protect them from flies. If, however, they are for human consumption, the rack may be covered over with canvas and the sides enclosed with frame planks, sheet metal strips, or sections of heavy cardboard. Then a slow fire of green wood, built in half an oil drum, is kept going in order to help dry the fish more quickly in wet weather and to keep off the flies. Fish that are only half dried may be boiled and eaten with seal oil that is obtained during the summer from Togiak people or permanent residents of Nushagak Bay.

As indicated in Chapter IV, nearly all Nushagak River men participate in the commercial fishery as fishermen and not as cannery workers. This means that they either own, or are in the process of buying, large fishing boats, or that they work on the boats usually assisting fathers, brothers, or other relatives. These boats are frequently obtained through the canneries, but some fishermen have purchased them with the aid of an organization known as the Tonuak Indian Credit Association, the only Indian credit association in Alaska. This organization, which was set up with the assistance and facilities of the Bureau of Indian Affairs through the efforts of a few mixed-bloods from the Dillingham area, borrows money from the United States government and re-lends it to the members for their economic improvement. Membership is open to all "Indians," in this case Eskimos, who have one-quarter or more "Indian" blood and who reside in the Nushagak and Togiak watersheds and the area in between. The capital stock at the time of incorporation in 1952 consisted of 3,000 shares at $10.00 each.

From the beginning the members of the association realized that the real economic need of the Eskimos in the area was for power fishing boats and fishing gear. They would then be able to improve other aspects of their economy. At the time of incorporation the original members estimated that a minimum of fifty power boats would supply the needs of the area. At that time it was thought that $7,500 would be the amount of a typical loan, but since 1952 the price of boats and equipment has doubled and the largest outstanding loan at the present time is more than $13,000. When the organization was established, ten loans were projected for the first year and the number was to be increased gradually. In 1965 there were sixty loans and the association had 125 members.

One of the purposes behind the Tonuak Indian Credit Association was, of course, to make the Eskimo fishermen truly independent by freeing them to some extent of their almost total dependency on the canneries. Generally, however, members of the association have gone to the canneries to borrow the down payments that are required and thus they are still bound to a particular cannery until the loan is repaid.

This study is not intended to deal exhaustively with the part the Nushagak River Eskimos play in the Bristol Bay salmon fishery. It is sufficient to note that most men are associated with the Pacific American Fisheries cannery at Dillingham, although a few work for other canneries in the bay region. The men live aboard their boats and are usually on the fishing grounds for long periods during open fishing periods. During the peak of the red salmon run the closed periods are frequent and the boats return to tie up at the cannery or in the small boat harbor. At this time the men may visit their families or enjoy the limited recreational facilities of Dillingham. As the season progresses, and particularly after the peak runs have passed, there are few if any closed periods, and the fishermen may simply fish for a while, returning to town whenever they happen to feel like it. This usually means that most of the boats are tied up over the weekends.

Although the cannery worker's minimum income is set by negotiations between the union and the canneries before the beginning of each fishing season, the fisherman has no guarantee of a minimum wage for his summer's work. The union does negotiate a price per fish for the different species of salmon at the beginning of each season. Thus the fisherman's income depends almost exclusively on the size of the run and his success at taking fish during the fishing periods. The red salmon runs are the most profitable and the success that a fisherman enjoys during a particular season depends heavily on his ability and opportunity to take red salmon. The price paid for reds was $1.09 each during the 1964 and 1965 fishing seasons. In recent years the prices paid for fish have been high but the runs have not always been remarkable for their size.

Many Nushagak River men took no more than 3,000 to 4,000 fish in 1964 and about 5,000 to 6,000 in 1965. This means that the "average" Eskimo fisherman made between $2,500 and $4,000 in a fair year such as 1964, more in a rather good year such as 1965. Some men, however, are extremely efficient and successful fishermen with good equipment. A New Koliganek man reported that he caught 12,000 red salmon in 1964 when he fished only for that species; this means that his income was in excess of $13,000. The following year he took 20,000 fish but nearly half this number were dog salmon so he probably made about $15,000. It should be remembered, however, that nearly all Nushagak fishermen owe large amounts on their boats, part of which they try to pay off every year. When the fishing season is poor, they often have difficulty paying the interests on their loans. The above New Koliganek man has a boat that cost approximately $12,000. In 1965 he made a payment of $5,000, but he has been making payments on the boat for seven years even though he is always one of the "high boats" of his cannery.

Considering the money that can be earned from commercial

fishing, it is not surprising that there is a great deal of speculation at the beginning of each season concerning the possible size of the red salmon run, and that local fishermen are quite reluctant to engage in any other activity during the fishing season. Aside from the investments represented by their boats and gear, the lure of the fishing season, the possibility of a fabulous run, etc. are very difficult to renounce even for the security associated with a less spectacular but more profitable form of employment.

During the summer of 1964 the Bureau of Indian Affairs began to construct a school at the new site chosen for the village of Koliganek: on the west bank of the river about four miles below the present village. Many Koliganek men could have found work on the school project, but few took advantage of the offer in spite of the relatively high wages. The Bureau paid a basic rate of $3.61 an hour to laborers and time and a half for work on Saturday. This meant that men employed there could earn in excess of $200 a week and also qualify for unemployment compensation during the winter which would amount to $45.00 per week plus $5.00 for every child in the recipient's family. In spite of this favorable situation, which was almost certain to mean a greater income for the workers than was likely to be earned by fishing, the foreman was never able to persuade more than half a dozen men to join the project. Instead, it was necessary to bring Indians over from a village on the Yukon. Of course some Koliganek men had obligations to the canneries that forced them to fish rather than take a construction job. But the lure of a possible big red salmon run was more than most fishermen were able to resist. Many desired to join the project, however, as soon as this valuable run was over, but by that time workers had been brought from elsewhere to fill the jobs.

In this brief review of subsistence activities practiced by contemporary inhabitants of the Nushagak River region, the emphasis has been exclusively on those Eskimos actually living along the river today. Of course, a sizable number of Eskimos also live the year round on Nushagak Bay, particularly in Dillingham. However, with the exception of some fall hunting and summer subsistence fishing, these people do not participate in anything that could conceivably be called a seasonal cycle of subsistence activities. A few men have full-time jobs and lead a life that is little different from that led by white residents of Dillingham. Others may work occasionally during the winter months but have no steady income apart from that they may earn during the summer fishing season. Both groups are part of an urbanized population that has very little contact with a traditional Eskimo way of life and that resembles, to a greater or lesser degree, similar populations in other cosmopolitan trading centers, such as Kotzebue, Point Barrow, and Bethel, which have grown up in Alaska. As in these other centers, the Eskimo population of Dillingham is to a large degree an economically depressed element of the total population, having tenuous ties to their villages of origin, but involved, at best, only marginally in the community where they live.

The importance of subsistence activities in the Nushagak River region has declined steadily, particularly during the last twenty or thirty years. This decline has now reached the point where it can probably be said that the people of the region are as much removed from traditional subsistence patterns as any group of Eskimos in Alaska outside of urban areas. Even trapping, which although not a traditional subsistence activity was nevertheless an important aspect of the economy during the early contact period, no longer plays a truly major part in the yearly economic cycle.

The salmon canneries have been primarily responsible for the decline of subsistence activities. The relatively high incomes that can be earned during the summer months have made it possible for many families to subsist through the winter with only marginal involvement in hunting and trapping. This has been particularly true since the Second World War when, as we have noted, Eskimo participation in the fishing industry increased to the point where all adult males are normally involved. The use of powered fishing boats after 1951 has not only been a major factor in the increase in Eskimo participation, but has also greatly affected the mobility of river people. Their contacts with Dillingham and with other river villages have become more frequent, and the acculturation process has consequently been speeded up considerably. At the same time, trapping has declined and multiple factors are doubtless involved here. Declining fur prices have affected Nushagak trappers as they have trappers all over northern North America. The fact that the area was closed to beaver trapping for so long a time undoubtedly resulted in a definite decline in interest in that activity; and even today, when that animal can once more be taken, the limit is so restricted that a man cannot make a living as a trapper. This kind of marginal involvement inevitably results in loss of interest and only desultory participation in the activity. Many Eskimos have found that with income derived from summer fishing, credit against the next season's earnings, a certain amount of hunting and fishing, and unearned income from various sources, they can subsist during the year. Thus it is not surprising to find that many people are interested in subsistence activities and trapping only to the extent that these are necessary in order to live from one fishing season to the next.

Of course subsistence fishing and a certain amount of moose hunting and the taking of small game and birds are still an important aspect of life on the Nushagak. Dogs must be fed through the winter months and the people themselves still rely heavily on fish put up during the summer and early fall. However, the hunting, fishing, and trapping practiced today is a far cry from the old settlement pattern involving summer residence on the river or bay and winter movement throughout the interior. Power fishing boats may have increased mobility along the river, but the interior areas adjacent to it are virtually unknown to younger Eskimos at the present time.

The four villages along the Nushagak River today are all that remain of the much larger number in existence at the close of the nineteenth century. And the settlements that exist in the bay area represent a considerable change from the pattern in the early contact period. These communities will now be briefly described and an attempt will be made to reconstruct the growth or decline of each one by indicating, as accurately as possible, when people settled and where they came from, or why they departed. This information has been obtained partly from village census records and partly from informants.

Koliganek. The village of Koliganek, abandoned in the late summer of 1964, was located on the west bank of the Nushagak approximately ten miles below the mouth of the Nuyakuk River; it was actually located on a small slough about a quarter of a mile from the main channel. The country around the village site is extremely flat and covered with a dense growth of willows and alders, a few stubby birch, and an occasional spruce. In early June, 1964, the water in the slough was high and the houses nearest the riverbank were virtually flooded. The water had been higher earlier in the spring and nearly all the houses had been under water at one time or another. The frequent flooding seems to have been the major factor in the decision of the villagers to move to a new location approximately four miles down the river and on the opposite bank.

Eighteen houses made up the village, but only two were occupied at the time, since most of the inhabitants were either on the coast fishing or at the new site working on the Bureau of Indian Affairs school. The houses and caches were built close together and the village had a crowded appearance. Toward the rear of the settlement stood a small, one-room frame schoolhouse and a small Russian Orthodox church.

The Koliganek site was occupied only briefly. The village was established only about twenty years previously by former residents of Old Koliganek located near the mouth of the Nuyakuk River. The Old Koliganek site was abandoned because of a scarcity of firewood in the area, but most older informants thought that it was a mistake to move. The old site was far superior in every way to Koliganek which is why the village has once more shifted.

The first federal census to include Koliganek was that of 1950 when the population was 90 (United States Census of Population 1960. Alaska, Number of Inhabitants, 1960, p. 10). An annual census was taken by the school taacher beginning in 1954 when a Bureau of Indian Affairs school was established in the community. From 1954 to 1963 the population was as follows:

1954	65	1959	83
1955	71	1960	100
1956	83	1961	100
1957	94	1962	85
1958	83	1963	96

The population fluctuates a good deal, reflecting the generally high degree of mobility in the Nushagak River region that has been a notable feature throughout the historic period. Some families move to the bay for several years and then return. It is not uncommon for a family to have a cabin in more than one community. In 1963 a number of Koliganek families moved to the mouth of Portage Creek where a new community had been established in that year.

Of the 31 family heads and their wives resident at Koliganek in 1963, 12 were born either in the village or at Old Koliganek, 2 in Ekwok, and the others in a variety of coastal settlements. From this it would appear that the upriver population has been growing slowly since Old Koliganek was abandoned in the early 1940's and that most of this additional population came from the coast. Nevertheless, a solid core of upriver people have lived in the area for at least a generation and probably longer. The yearly fluctuations in population do not obscure this basic fact. The interesting thing is that in spite of temporary movements of Koliganek people to the coast, the village appears to have grown at the expense of the coastal population in recent years.

New Koliganek. The site chosen for the new village is on the west bank of the river about four miles below the present village. Here the bank is high and the ground relatively dry and level. The timber is not heavy, but the Eskimos are not so dependent on it as they were previously and with their fast, large power boats, building logs and firewood can easily be brought from other locations along the river. The Bureau of Land Management has surveyed the new site and each family has a 100 by 100 foot lot for a cabin. Four cabins were started during the summer of 1964 and by August, 1965, thirteen had been constructed and there were approximately 100 people living in the new village. Some families cut new logs for their houses, while others salvaged all or part of their old dwellings at Koliganek. The church was brought down to the new site in the fall of 1965. When the Bureau of Indian Affairs began construction of a $350,000 school during the summer of 1964, a small number of Koliganek men, as well as workers from other places, worked on this project throughout that summer and most of the summer of 1965.

The cabins at New Koliganek, stretching for the most part in a single row along the riverbank, are typical of those in all Nushagak River communities. They are of chinked log construction with split logs being used for the roofs. Old cannery sheet metal sometimes covers the split logs and sod may be placed on top of the metal; most have split log floors. By each house is a log cache, usually standing well off the ground on four poles. The lower portion of some of the caches is closed in to be used as a tool and equipment shed, while dry fish and other food may be kept in the top part. All houses have small storm sheds and these are also used for storage.

The smallest cabins are about eighteen feet square and some of the larger ones are twenty by twenty feet. The interior walls are frequently covered with cardboard for insulation and the larger houses are sometimes partitioned into smaller rooms or plywood halfwalls are built up around one or more of the beds to give a certain amount of privacy. Interior furnishings include heavy frame beds or iron cots covered with mattresses, sleeping bags, and quilts. In corners and under the beds clothing and personal items are stored in cardboard suitcases and large boxes. On the walls hang religious pictures and calendars. Some people heat their houses with stove oil, but most use wood and have cooking ranges of varying degrees of antiquity. Light is generally provided by pressure lamps, although one man has an electric light plant that serves eight houses and for which he charges the residents of each $5.00 per year. Radios and gas washing machines are common in the village. By the fall of 1965, only two steam baths had been constructed. New Koliganek lacks one feature that is characteristic of the older Nushagak River villages; there are no old fishing boats in varying stages of disrepair lying about.

Generally speaking, the people of New Koliganek seem pleased with the new location of their village and particularly with their new school. Apparently before the move there were a few people who favored returning to the Old Koliganek site, but it was generally felt that this was too remote.

New Stuyahok. The village of New Stuyahok is located on the west bank of the Nushagak, approximately forty river miles below Koliganek south of the mouth of a small creek that flows into the river at this point. The creek valley broadens as it reaches the river and the village is situated in a broad, flat area between two widely spaced hills. An impressive federal school, constructed in 1960, stands on a hillside to the south of the village. The settlement consists of twenty-eight houses, most of them of logs, but two or three of frame construction. These houses, situated close to one another, vary considerably in size and the whole village presents a cluttered appearance because of the many out-buildings: four or five steam baths and many caches, sheds, smokehouses, fish drying racks, and outhouses. Some of the houses have their own light plants and there is a community-owned sawmill. In the northwest corner of the village stands a Russian Orthodox church and next to it is a small cemetery.

New Stuyahok was included in the federal census for the first time in 1950 when the population was 88 (U.S. Census of Popula-tion 1960. Alaska, Number of Inhabitants, 1960, p. 11). The vil-lage appears to have been established about 1940 and the earliest inhabitants, as the name implies, came from the settlement of Stuyahok—or Old Stuyahok as it is sometimes called—on the Mul-chatna River. It seems certain that New Stuyahok was small at first but it grew rapidly and was augmented, in the 1940's, by people moving down from Nunachuak. After the school was es-tablished in 1954 a yearly census was taken by the Bureau of In-dian Affairs teacher, and the figures are as follows:

1954	108	1957	114	1960	140
1955	101	1958	123	1961	147
1956	107	1959	133	1962	172

New Stuyahok grew rapidly after 1955 and is now by far the larg-est village on the river. The rapid recent growth is doubtless part-ly due to the large new school that opened in the fall of 1960. The extent to which the settlement has drawn on other communities in the area for population is illustrated by the following list of com-munities in which New Stuyahok family heads and their wives were born:

Ekwok	4	Old Stuyahok	6	Snake River	1
Nunachuak	8	Togiak	2	Mulchatna River	2
Kanakanak	3	Dillingham	4	Koliganek	2
Nushagak	3	Platinum	1	Igushik	3
Wood River Village	6	Kokwok	1	Angle Bay	1

This list is based on the population in 1962 and it shows that New Stuyahok, the most recent of the Nushagak villages, has drawn upon the entire river region and Nushagak Bay for its population. Nevertheless, the village retains a core of families whose former home was the Mulchatna River and it also seems to have absorbed the final inhabitants of Nunachuak. In spite of its cosmopolitan population, then, the settlement has basic continuity with the middle river and its inhabitants.

Ekwok. This community, situated about seventeen miles below New Stuyahok on the same side of the river, was established probably in the last decade of the nineteenth century, and is the oldest continuously occupied village on the Nushagak River. It grew rapidly, apparently at the expense of the nearby settlements of Kokwok and Akulivikchuk and by 1923 Ekwok was the largest settlement along the river.

The village is located about a quarter of a mile north of a small stream that flows into the river. A relatively low, flat area stretches north of this stream and then rises rather abruptly to form a high bank. Toward the west the stream valley slopes up gradually and there is a low ridge about a quarter of a mile behind the village. Ekwok differs from the other communities along the river in that it is spread out over a wide area. Six houses, along with caches and fish racks, stand on the bank of the river in the flat area closest to the stream. Five are situated directly in back of these and on the slope that rises gently to the west. Six dwellings are scattered along the high ridge to the north. Probably not all of these are currently occupied, some having been built in the past by white men. As late as 1932, according to one resident, all houses were located in the low, flat area along the riverbank. In late June, 1964, the settlement was virtually deserted; all the men were on the coast and only a few families were left behind to put up dry fish. Old cabin sites occur throughout the village indicating that it was once soemwhat larger than at present. Along the bank of the river in the flat area there is about a foot and a half of midden, at the base of which a number of tin cans and other debris are weathering out. Only the cabins at the high point of the slope to the west and on the northern ridge are free from the possibility of flooding. Ekwok has three churches: a Russian Orthodox, a Church of Christ which has apparently been inactive for many years, and a Seventh Day Adventist church. All are located on the northern ridge as is the state school which was established in 1932. In 1930 the village received a post office which at one time served the entire river.

Ekwok is the last in a line of important mid-river settlements

The Nushagak River Today   149

that made this the most populous region of the Nushagak
throughout most of the historic period. Ekwok may have grown
rapidly in the 1920's but in 1930, the first year the village appears
in the federal census, the population was only 40 (Fifteenth Census of the United States: 1930, vol. 1, 1930, p. 1222). It still may
have been the largest village on the river since Old Koliganek
was declining by this time and New Stuyahok was not yet in existence. Nunachuak had a population of 32 the same year and the
river population as a whole, not including the Mulchatna, must
have been very low. A yearly census was taken at Ekwok by the
Bureau of Indian Affairs between 1932 and 1954 when the school
was turned over to the territory. These figures do not seem particularly trustworthy nor do they correspond to the federal figures.
Nevertheless they suggest that the village grew slowly in the
1930's and early 1940's, reaching a peak about 1946 when there
were 100 inhabitants. Then the population slipped again until in
1964 there were approximately 75 permanent residents. The federal census figures seem consistently too high, the population in
1939 being listed as 68, in 1950 as 131, and 106 in 1960 (United
States Census of Population 1960. Alaska, Number of Inhabitants,
1960, p. 10). In 1940 and again in 1950 the census material collected by the schoolteacher shows the birthplace of family heads
and this gives some idea of the areas from which Ekwok was
drawing its population.

1940 census		1950 census	
Kanakanak	1	Kolukuk	1
Ugashik	3	Stuyahok	1
Dillingham	4	Kanakanak	1
Ekwok	6	Wood River Village	1
Nushagak	1	Ekwok	3
Kokwok	3	Dillingham	4
False Pass (Aleut)	1	Kanulik	1
Togiak	1	Kokwok	1
		Koliganek	1

By 1940, the village was already drawing much of its population
from coastal points, a trend that was even more noticeable ten
years later. The middle river influence, doubtless strong immediately after the community was established, has largely disappeared by 1940 and was even less noticeable in 1950. In fact,
three of the six family heads born in Ekwok had either died or

moved away. The situation suggests that Ekwok, like Koliganek–
New Koliganek and New Stuyahok, has been drawing on the
coast for its population in the last twenty-five years.

Portage Creek. A village has grown up at the mouth of Portage
Creek since 1963-64. During the winter of 1964-65 eleven families
lived there and it was expected that at least five more houses
would be built in the late fall of 1965. This would make Portage
Creek almost equal in size to Ekwok and New Koliganek. It is
likely that people have camped at this point from time to time in
the past since Portage Creek, as the name implies, is part of a
route that enabled people to move easily in summer from the
head of Nushagak Bay to the mouth of the Kvichak River without
exposing themselves to the open waters of Bristol Bay and the
trip around Etolin Point. The vital statistics records in the office
of the Deputy Magistrate in Dillingham record deaths at Portage
Creek in 1933 and 1934.

Many of the residents of the new Portage Creek community
have come from Koliganek, but there is also a growing number of
families from Dillingham. The location of the village is attractive
to those people who, for various reasons, do not wish to live in
the metropolitan center but, at the same time, do not want to be
too far away. Informants maintained that the trip from Portage
Creek to Dillingham by dog team could be made in less than five
hours and it is, of course, a much quicker trip by boat. Western
Alaska Airlines, the local scheduled carrier, began a regular service into the community in 1965. Within the next few years Portage Creek may grow at the expense of other villages in the
Nushagak River region.

Clark's Point. The village of Clark's Point, less than two miles
north of Ekuk on Nushagak Bay, closely resembles the latter
community in that it too is strung out along a spit that has been
formed by wave action and has a cannery at the north end of the
spit. There are about thirty residences, mostly of frame and sheet
metal construction, with a few tents. The spit is much shorter
than the one at Ekuk, being less than a mile in length. Consequently the houses are much closer together. There is a Moravian
church in the village as well as a new state school.

The occupation of Clark's Point goes back at least to the end of
the nineteenth century and in the sources of that period the point

has an Eskimo name, Stugarok. No sign of an old site was observed on the bluff in back of the village, although the examination was cursory and not all possible locations were examined. However, the Russian sources make no mention of an Eskimo community at this location and it is perhaps logical that there would be no village so close to the large Ekuk settlement. In 1888 the Nushagak Packing Company established a cannery at Stugarok and the resulting settlement appears in the Eleventh Census, at which time it had a population of 7 living in one house (Moser, 1899, pp. 173-174; Porter, 1893, pp. 93-94, 164). The community is named for John W. Clark, manager of the Alaska Commercial Company store at Nushagak until his death in 1897, who is said to have operated a saltery on the spit before the cannery was established (Malach, 1950, p. 7). The settlement does not appear in the federal census until 1930 at which time it had a population of 25 (Fifteenth Census of the United States: 1930, vol. 1, Population, 1931, p. 1222). In 1939 the figure was 22, but the population rose abruptly to 128 in 1950, and to 138 in 1960 (United States Census of Population 1960. Alaska, Number of Inhabitants, 1960, p. 10).

Clark's Point appears never to have been anything but a cannery town which, until the past few years, attracted Eskimos only during the summer months when the cannery was in operation or, more recently, used as a fishing station. In recent years a small permanent population, at least sufficient to warrant the establishment of a school and mission, appears to have grown up. This population has, for the most part, been drawn from other communities on Nushagak Bay, although a few families from the river communities and from other settlements in the Bristol Bay region may also have settled there.

Ekuk. The village of Ekuk today, as opposed to the archaeological site, is located along a narrow gravel spit that extends out from the Ekuk Bluffs in the form of a hook. Behind the series of gravel beaches toward the high country to the east is an area of dense marsh grass interspersed with sloughs. The village itself, of approximately thirty houses and tents, is strung out along the spit for a distance of one and one-half or two miles. At the extreme north end of the spit is an operating cannery. At the other end, on the bluff, is the old site as well as a Russian Orthodox church and graveyard. There is also a state school in the settlement. The houses at Ekuk are all of frame and tarpaper construction, or made of sheet metal taken from old cannery buildings.

At one time Ekuk was a sizable and important Eskimo village, and an old one too since the earliest Russian accounts mention it (Khromchenko, 1824). In 1960 the official census gives a population of 40 for the community and it is doubtful whether this figure has been much exceeded at any time since the late nineteenth century (United States Census of Population 1960. Alaska, Number of Inhabitants, 1960, p. 10). Today Ekuk is little more than a cannery town with a large summer population of fishermen and cannery workers. Few families spend the entire year in the village. In fact, in the late summer of 1964, informants were saying that they doubted whether more than three or four families, including the cannery caretaker, would be staying in the village during the coming winter.

Most of the people in Ekuk during the summer are from villages on the Nushagak, from Togiak, Aleknagik, and other Bristol Bay locations. They have cabins in Ekuk, but they use them only in summer and refer to them as summer camps. Typical of the summer residents is a family from New Koliganek who have a comfortable two-room cabin made of old cannery sheet metal. This family comes to Ekuk late in May each year; and while the father drift nets with his boat and sells fish to the cannery, his wife operates a set net from a registered location and also sells her catch.

It can be seen, therefore, that the original Ekuk population has been dispersed and that there really is no true coastal population, at least in this part of Nushagak Bay. However, it is perhaps no exaggeration to make this statement for the entire bay region. What exists at Ekuk, for example, is a temporary summer population from up the river and from other Bristol Bay points that includes a few families which, for one reason or another, make Ekuk their permanent home. To some extent, the same is true for Dillingham although the situation for that community is more complex and there appears also to be remnants of a coastal population living there. At any rate, Ekuk is no longer a functioning community with its own organization and sense of identity and continuity with the past.

Dillingham-Kanakanak. Previously mention has been made of the fact that the Dillingham area has emerged as the largest and most important town in the Nushagak River region and one of the largest in southwestern Alaska. We have noted the normal gravitation of population and economic activity to a single point as the area developed, and we have also noted the growth of the salmon canning industry in the immediate vicinity of Dillingham. Other causes are directly related to the fact that Dillingham has emerged as a large and important economic and trading center. Its size means that it offers better community facilities than are available elsewhere in the area. Since the advent and expansion of air travel, families have found it feasible to establish homes at the center where the best education, health, and community services are available, while continuing to exploit the natural resources in other parts of the region (Rogers, 1955, p. 6). This has been true to a limited extent for Eskimos as well as for whites.

Today the Dillingham-Kanakanak population complex is closely associated with the Dillingham road system, the most significant portion of which stretches from Kanakanak to Dillingham, a distance of approximately seven miles. At Kanakanak is the United States Public Health Service hospital that provides medical and dental care for the native population of the Bristol Bay region. There is a small community and church in the Kanakanak area and several houses are built along the road toward Dillingham. However, Kanakanak, as late as 1930 a sizable town, has declined in importance as the population has gravitated toward the larger center. About halfway along the road is the Dillingham airport, maintained by the Federal Aviation Administration, and on the west side of Dillingham is the former municipal airport now used only by small planes. Indicative of the growth in importance of Dillingham is the fact that it is now served by daily flights from Anchorage as well as by frequent scheduled flights to and from King Salmon, Togiak, and other Bristol Bay points.

Approaching Dillingham from the southwest in summer, one encounters a small tent camp of Eskimos. These are people from Aleknagik, Togiak, and other Bristol Bay points who have come to work in the cannery. The town itself lies at the foot of a steep bluff and is dominated by the buildings of the Pacific American Fisheries, the only cannery operating in the immediate Dillingham area. The abandoned "Scandanavian" cannery stands about a quarter of a mile south of the operating one. Immediately to the north of the cannery buildings is the commercial center of Dillingham. Here are two general merchandise stores, the offices of Western Alaska Airlines, a new post office building also housing apartments and the offices of Northern Consolidated Airlines, a filling station, and a movie theater. Other commercial establishments in the town include a branch of the National Bank of Alaska, a hardware and variety store, a grocery and market, a bakery, three package liquor stores, two restaurants, a snack bar, two pool halls, two bars, and two hotels. Two scheduled airlines and six charter flying services operate in Dillingham.

Churches in the Dillingham area include the Seventh Day Adventist, Church of Christ, Moravian, Baptist, Roman Catholic, and Russian Orthodox. A full-time physician and surgeon conducts a private practice and maintains a small clinic. A public health nurse is in residence too. A new high school building was constructed in 1961 and there are public school buildings at the north end of town. Also in the area is a Roman Catholic mission school affording education to the high school level and a Seventh Day Adventist school in which nine grades are taught.

Telephone service is provided to the residents of Dillingham and vicinity by the Trans-Alaska Telephone Company and includes both local and long distance service. A diesel-electric generating plant operated by the Dillingham Public Utility District provides power and light; and it supplies electricity as far as Aleknagik, about twenty-five miles to the north. A sewer system and sewage disposal plant was completed in the summer of 1964.

Southwest of town is a small boat harbor for the area's fishing fleet. This was completed in 1962 by the United States Army Corp of Engineers. Dillingham's road system is limited to about thirty-five miles of gravel road that includes a twenty-five mile stretch to Aleknagik.

Although there seems to be no specific section of Dillingham where Eskimos live, a group of frame shacks along the beach north of the center of town seem, for the most part, to be occupied by people whose winter homes are in other villages. Some are from Aleknagik and others from the Nushagak settlements, while some of the shacks are occupied the year round by families who now consider Dillingham to be their permanent home. North of these shacks on the beach at the foot of the bluff known as Snag Point is another tent village inhabitated mostly by people from New Koliganek. Near each tent is a rack for drying fish. The rack is usually covered with sections of scrap sheet iron to protect the fish against the rain. Some of the men keep their fishing boats drawn up on the beach in front of the tents. The women tend set nets and put up dry fish while the men are fishing for the cannery. This tent village, which was a thriving settlement in the summer of 1963, was virtually deserted in 1964 when some New Koliganek families stayed upriver to work on the new school. (The New Stuyahok people tend to camp at Lewis Point, while Ekwok families either remain in the village or camp at the mouth of a small creek north of the old Wood River Village site.)

This brief description of the Dillingham region can be concluded by noting that governmental agencies located in the town, and responsible for much of the available employment, include the United States Public Health Service Hospital at Kanakanak, the Federal Aviation Administration, the United States Fish and Wildlife Service, the Alaska Department of Fish and Game, the Alaska Division of Highways, the Alaska State Police, an office of the United States Deputy Magistrate, and the United States Public Health Service nurse.

In the federal census for 1930, Dillingham and Kanakanak were listed separately, with a population of 85 given for the former and 177 for the latter (Fifteenth Census of the United States: 1930, vol. 1, Population, 1931, p. 1222). After that the figures for the two communities were combined but there is no doubt that shortly after 1930 Dillingham began to grow rapidly at the expense of its southern neighbor. In 1939, the population was 278, in 1950 it rose to 577 and declined to 424 in 1960 (United States Census of Population 1960. Alaska, Number of Inhabitants, 1960, p. 10). These figures must be viewed with reservations as it cannot be ascertained at what time of the year the data were collected. During the summer months well over 1,000 people reside in the Dillingham area, while the permanent winter population in recent years has probably been close to 500.

Aleknagik. The Eskimo population of the Lake Aleknagik region was virtually wiped out by the influenza epidemic of 1918-1919 with the few survivors, mostly infants, moving or being taken elsewhere. Only since around 1928 have people begun to filter back into the area. In that year an Eskimo family moved to the southeast end of Lake Aleknagik from the Togiak region and it appears to have been the first of many families, mostly from this general area, particularly from Kulukak, to move to the lake. Slightly later Frank Waskey, a noted Alaskan and the Territory's first delegate to Congress, moved to the lake and established a small colony of Seventh Day Adventists which began to grow slowly. The new community appears in the vital statistics of the Nushagak Church in 1930, suggesting that a sizable Eskimo population was beginning to form. There are also some Kuskokwim people on the lake.

In 1930 and 1931 Mertie noted that as many as 40 white people lived at the east end of the lake and that a post office called Aleknagik had recently been established (Mertie, 1938, pp. 24-26). By 1940 the Seventh Day Adventist colony numbered 60 inhabitants and there were about thirty buildings, a sawmill, school, and church in the area (Anonymous, 1941, p. 19). A state school was established in 1945 or 1946.

As early as 1930-1931 a road between Dillingham and Aleknagik was planned which was to go by way of the Wood River cannery. The first leg of this road, as far as the cannery, was completed in the early 1930's but not until the last few years was the Aleknagik road, which proceeds by a different route, finally finished. The white community at Aleknagik continued to grow, perhaps until the 1950's, and after that declined as more families moved either to Dillingham or to the southern forty-eight states. The Eskimo community also continued to grow and at present there are some 35 Eskimo families scattered around the eastern end of the lake. There are now Moravian and Russian Orthodox churches at the lake as well as the Seventh Day Adventist church and mission school, the latter constructed around 1945. Not until 1960, however, were the inhabitants of the area enumerated in a federal census. In the census for that year two communities are listed: Aleknagik Lake with a population of 181, and Aleknagik Mission with 50 inhabitants (United States Census of Population 1960. Alaska, Number of Inhabitants, 1960, p. 10). The former figure suggests the extent to which the area has become a new center for an inland Eskimo population.

X

Comparative Summary and Conclusions

◇◆◇

STUDENTS OF ALASKAN ESKIMO CULTURE HAVE LONG BEEN AWARE of the fact that the precontact way of life in their area has never been so well documented ethnographically as that of central Canada and Greenland. Charles Hughes has pointed out that in spite of the pioneer work by some of the Russian missionaries and explorers and American natural historians of the late nineteenth century, nothing in the literature of aboriginal Alaskan Eskimo culture compares with the monumental ethnographies of Boas, Jenness, and members of the Fifth Thule Expedition (Hughes, 1965, p. 27). As Hughes has suggested, good historical reasons account for this unequal situation. The Eskimo cultures of the eastern Arctic remained relatively uninfluenced by external forces until the period of modern ethnographic fieldwork in the 1920's, while most of the Alaskan Eskimo groups had already undergone profound changes by the end of the nineteenth century (Hughes, 1965, pp. 27-28). Some Alaskan ethnographers, notably Rainey, Lantis, and Giddings, were remarkably successful in reconstructing precontact culture, but in recent years anthropologists in the western Arctic have focused almost entirely on modern Eskimo communities and problems of culture change. There seems to be a general feeling that the reconstruction of ethnography is no longer profitable or even possible.

The current interest in modern Eskimo communities, however, has also focused the attention of some Arctic specialists on the

historical process of change. Since modern Eskimo culture represents the current end point in the history of culture change, it has
been realized that this culture, as studied at the present time, is
meaningful only in terms of what can be learned about the earlier
periods of the cultural continuum. With this in mind, ethnographers are beginning to realize that a wealth of historical materials
exists for the early period of contact between Eskimos and Europeans in Alaska and some students are using the techniques of archaeology not only as a key to an understanding of the remote
past, but as an extension of ethnography and history, an important research method for reconstructing the impact of an alien
culture on the nienteenth-century Eskimos.

In the introduction to this study it was pointed out that cultural
historical studies of the type presented here should be considered
as basic to the studies of present-day peoples and communities.
This would seem to be particularly true for an area which, like
Alaska, lacks a well documented ethnographic baseline on which
to build the study of modern communities and problems of culture change. The fact that a large number of the current studies
of Eskimo communities make some attempt to place their data
within an historic framework is an implicit recognition of this
fact. Because of growing attention to the historical context of
change, it is both possible and desirable to consider the data for
the Nushagak River region from a comparative standpoint and to
draw some broad parallels based upon what we know of nineteenth-century contact between Eskimos and Europeans in other
areas of Alaska. The emphasis in this comparative treatment will
be on the Kuskokwim River region and the coast of Alaska north
of Kotzebue Sound.

Russian and American exploration in the Nushagak River region was discussed in the first chapter of this study. It was noted
that the establishment of Alexandrovski Redoubt and the subsequent penetration of the interior was intrinsically connected with
the fur trade and that, by the middle of the nineteenth century,
much of southwestern Alaska had at least been roughly mapped
and the inhabitants brought within the orbit of various coastal
and interior trading posts. In northwestern Alaska, the basic
coastal exploration took place somewhat earlier but the interior
regions remained virtually unexplored until the end of the centu-

ry. At the same time, the rationale for exploration along the northern coasts was different from that which motivated those Russians who penetrated the interior river systems between the Yukon and the Nushagak. Cook and Kotzebue were concerned primarily with increasing geographical knowledge, while Beechey was associated with Sir John Franklin's explorations of the Mackenzie region. These navigators, along with the later European and American explorers involved in the search for Franklin's third expedition, affected the Eskimo population only slightly. In fact, they had little or no interest in the local inhabitants aside from the possibility that they could supply information, food, and water.

When we consider missionary activity in the two areas, even greater discrepancy, both in time and in intensity of contact can be noted. In the Nushagak River region Russian Orthodox missionaries followed closely on the heels of the trade-oriented explorers, and by the middle of the century all the Eskimos had at least a superficial acquaintance with the Orthodox brand of Christianity. The same can be said of the vast Yukon-Kuskokwim area. In northwest Alaska, on the other hand, the people were almost completely unacquainted with Christianity until virtually the end of the century. It is likely, however, that in this area, the missionaries had a greater initial impact because they frequently opened schools and offered medical services in connection with their mission work (VanStone, 1964). Because the villages of northwest Alaska were less scattered than those along the river systems of the southwest, the missionaries could reach a greater proportion of the population more regularly and more effectively. In fact, most of the villages of the northwest had a resident missionary almost constantly after 1890, while neither the Russian Orthodox priests nor the Moravians were able to achieve the same intensity of exposure among the scattered and more mobile populations of the Yukon, Kuskokwim, and Nushagak regions. In both areas, however, the time was propitious for all kinds of changes as the Eskimos were drawn increasingly into a trapping-trading economy (Oswalt, 1963, pp. 153-154; VanStone, 1964). It is probably true, then, that although missionary activity began much earlier in the southwest and the missionaries played a vital and lasting role as agents of change during most of the nine-

teenth century, the end result in the two areas is roughly comparable because of the more intensive relations between Eskimos
and their spiritual advisors in the north.

The Russian-American Company, as we have seen, was established in the Nushagak River region in the second decade of the
nineteenth century. Within thirty years it had opened up all of
southwestern Alaska to the fur trade. A relatively small number
of individuals carried out this expansion, and they appear to have
established their role among the people with caution. They had
no force to back up their position and thus could not afford to op-
pose the people as they had been able to do in the Aleutians and
throughout southeastern Alaska. The Russians apparently did not
interfere in the affairs of the various southwest Alaskan villages
with which they had contact and usually they did not establish
their major trading stations in occupied villages (Oswalt, 1963, p.
106). Along the Kuskokwim River, archaeological excavations
have shown that Russian influence on Eskimo material culture
was relatively minor (Oswalt and VanStone, 1967) and there is
every indication that the same was also true for the Nushagak.

The purchase of Alaska by the United States did not alter the
basic relationship between the Eskimos and traders in southwestern Alaska, although the number and variety of trade goods entering the region appears to have increased. By this time, however, agents of change other than the trader were beginning to
exert their influence.

In northwest Alaska the Eskimos had access to trade goods at
an even earlier date than in the southwestern region. By the middle of the seventeenth century the Russians had penetrated north-
eastern Siberia, and European goods began to flow into Alaska
from the Chukchi and the Siberian Eskimos by way of the people
of the Diomede Islands and Cape Prince of Wales. As early as the
beginning of the eighteenth century the people of the Diomedes
and Cape Prince of Wales became the middlemen of this inter-
continental trade; and trading centers, such as the one at Hotham
Inlet, became important distribution centers for all of northwest
Alaska (VanStone, 1962a, p. 126).

After 1850, commerical whalers began to frequent the Arctic
Ocean in large numbers every summer and from them the Eskimos first received trade goods in large quantities. The whalers,

who were interested in obtaining baleen, traded with the Eskimos for it and also took large quantities with their own ships; some Eskimos worked on the whaling vessels and at shore-based whaling stations. Eskimos in all the villages along the western Arctic coast were eager to obtain trade goods, and looked forward to the arrival of the whaling ships with great eagerness every spring. The people were paid in such items as flour, crackers, black tobacco, matches, lead rifles, ammunition, and molasses. (VanStone, 1958).

Toward the end of the nineteenth century, when the demand for baleen began to fall off, some whaling vessels found it profitable to combine trading with whaling, and the first regularly established trade contacts with northwest Alaska villages came about in this way. Thus traders were fixtures in some villages by the time whaling ended in the second decade of the present century (VanStone, 1960, p. 176).

It is impossible to consider the whole process of technological change comparatively without reference to the commercial fishing industry which, as we have seen, grew up in the Bristol Bay region toward the end of the nineteenth century and almost immediately began to influence the Eskimo inhabitants of the area. In many ways this industry parallels the development of commercial whaling in the north. Both were seasonal activities and agents of intensive change. Of course there are many differences. The commercial fishing industry has continued to be important in the area and has employed increasing numbers of Eskimos from throughout southwestern Alaska and other areas. It represented an earlier introduction to true wage employment than any commercial development in the north, and no period of adjustment was required paralleling the one that was necessary in northwest Alaska after the decline in baleen prices brought an end to the whaling industry. The commercial fishing industry also had a pronounced effect on settlement patterns in the Bristol Bay region, although there are no indications that other areas of southwestern Alaska were similarly affected. As the canneries grew up, flourished, declined, and were abandoned, they were directly responsible for population shifts in the bay area; while along the Nushagak River itself, traditional movements of people throughout the whole year were influenced by the fact that summer residence at or near a cannery was required. The whalers, on the other hand, were drawn to the Eskimo villages and although a certain coalescence of population took place during the summer months as a result of the presence of the whaling ships, no lasting changes in the settlement pattern occurred. The population groupings today along the north coast of Alaska are much the same as they were at the beginning of the contact period. In a sense, then, both whaling and commercial fishing represent attempts by the Eskimos of both areas to obtain trade goods through the barter of environmental products. Only in southwest Alaska, however, has this particular type of economic endeavor endured, and the economic history of the area to the present time has been conditioned to a large degree by attempts on the part of both Eskimos and other residents to achieve a greater and more profitable role in the harvest of this renewable resource.

When we consider miners as agents of change in southwestern Alaska we are forced to conclude that the record of known individuals searching for minerals throughout the whole area indicates that they were few in number and probably offered the Eskimo comparatively little in the way of trade goods. In northwest Alaska, the miners' influence cannot be dismissed quite so simply, although it is unlikely that they played a role comparable in any way to that of other agents of change. During the last few years of the nineteenth century, miners hoping to reach the gold fields frequently went north on the whaling ships and then deserted in Eskimo villages. Although some individuals spent a year of more in different communities, there is no indication that the knowledge of Euro-American material and social culture obtained by the Eskimos from these people in any way rivaled the influx of ideas and objects that were coming into the villages on the whaling ships.

We have noted that the people of the Nushagak River region participated only marginally in the reindeer herding program instituted by the Bureau of Education in 1892 for the benefit of northern Eskimos who were suffering from the decline in sea mammals caused by unrestricted killing of whales, walrus, and seals. Largely through the efforts of Moravian missionaries, the Kuskokwim Eskimos became involved in the reindeer program as early as 1901, but they served mainly as hired herders; and although large herds were involved in the beginning, it is doubtful whether the effects of the herding program were either extensive or long lasting. The basic skills of close herding were never learned well by the Eskimos of the region and the industry perished without having any effect on Eskimo life (Oswalt, 1963, pp. 46-47). In northwest Alaska the story was somewhat different, even though the program eventually failed there too. At Point Hope, for example, the reindeer herd served as the Eskimos' introduction to Euro-American economic methodology. After 1926, all deer owned by individual villagers were counted into a single herd owned by a joint stock company. A board of directors elected from among the shareholders ran the herd and a store as well. In the late 1920's the store separated from the reindeer herd, probably because the former was much more successful. But the tradition of a village-owned store persisted, and eventually it became affiliated with the Alaska Native Industries Cooperative Association and later a completely independent village-owned store (VanStone, 1962b, pp. 139-140). Unquestionably, the knowledge and skills gained through the operation of the reindeer company helped to prepare the Eskimos of Point Hope and other northern villages for a more sophisticated involvement in a new type of economic existence. This legacy has made the long defunct reindeer herding program a more significant agent of change in the north than in the south.

In discussing educational services in the Nushagak River region we noted that although some facilities were available there as long or even longer than in most other parts of Alaska, relatively few people were in a position to take advantage of them. Only in the last twenty-five years or so has education been generally available to the people living in interior villages. In the Kuskokwim and Yukon regions, inland penetration of educational facilities took place somewhat earlier than along the Nushagak, but again only within recent years has formal education played an important part in the life of young people in these regions. In northwest Alaska, on the other hand, education was firmly established in most villages by the first missionaries near the close of the nineteenth century, and government schools followed rapidly in the easily accessible coastal villages. Because of this solid foundation and the continuity of educational services, education has been a vital acculturative factor and young people are being drawn increasingly into the mainstream of American life by means of their involvement in formal education. At Point Hope, for example, in recent years all graduates of the eight grades taught in the village have attended the government high school at Mt. Edgecumbe, and a growing number have enrolled in specialized training courses at centers outside Alaska. Although this trend is also developing in the southern regions, it lags well behind similar developments in the north. Most village young people in the Nushagak area still take their places in the community following their graduation from local schools and only a few, notably from the Dillingham area, participate in the educational programs that are now generally available to the native peoples of Alaska.

The degree to which medical services have been provided to the Eskimos of Alaska varies considerably. In the north, some of the first missionaries were also men with medical training and they seem first to have gained the confidence of the people through their ability to cure illnesses and to free the people from their fear of shamans. In the southwestern area, medical missionaries also played an important role and although formal medical services sponsored by the government may have been introduced relatively late, they were able to build on the solid foundations laid by the earlier practitioners. Since Eskimos throughout Alaska were continually exposed to virulent epidemics throughout the period of contact, evidence in all areas suggests that the long experience which the Eskimos have had with introduced European diseases has conditioned them to accept unusual forms of treatment for unusual diseases from outsiders, particularly in comparison to many other areas of the world. Disease causation and the basic tenets of preventive medicine may be understood no better here than they are in other marignal areas, but people are usually willing to accept professional help to at least the partial exclusion of local traditional remedies.

Perhaps the most important single point to emerge from this comparative overview of the activities of agents of change throughout Alaska is the significance of the early penetration of the interior by these agents in southwestern Alaska. At the time the whalers were establishing the first intensive contacts with Eskimos in northern Alaska, the area between the Yukon and the

Nushagak was already well opened to the fur trade and to the influence of the Russian Orthodox Church. Because transportation between the coast and the interior was relatively easy in this region and game and fur-bearing animals continued to be plentiful, the interior was never depopulated nor did the communities experience a marked decline as coastal trading centers grew up. We have documented the profound effect that the activities of the various agents of change in the Nushagak region had on the subsistence pattern and, as a result, also on the settlement pattern, but interior communities tended to coalesce or move within the interior setting. This contrasts markedly to northwest Alaska where the entire arctic slope region was rapidly abandoned as a result of the intensive contacts established by agents of change in the coastal communities.

And yet in spite of the many differences affecting the pattern and rates of changes throughout Alaska north of the Alaska Peninsula, the end result does not reflect as many of these differences as might be expected. The acculturation level throughout the area under discussion is, everything considered, remarkably uniform.

At the same time, it seems worthwhile to stress the difference with reference to one basic fact of present day life: the extent to which people throughout Alaska have been drawn into a wage economy and the effect this has had on their traditional subsistence activities. Throughout their long history, the coastal villages of northwest Alaska have enjoyed the benefits of their location in one of the best sea mammal hunting areas in the world. Because of this almost complete dependence on sea mammals, subsistence activities in the coastal settlements closely reflect the movements of the sea ice and take on their characteristic cyclical pattern. A notable feature of this cycle has been the fact that the summer months, when the sea ice is absent from the vicinity of the villages, always have been a time of relative inactivity. Since the end of the Second World War, all of Alaska has been the scene of considerable construction activity, much of it in connection with defense installations and related projects. To an increasing degree, Eskimos have taken part in that work, most of which takes place during the summer months. Thus the people of the northern villages have been able to fit wage economy into the seasonal cycle at a time when little hunting is possible. As a result they have achieved a successful combination of traditional subsistence and wage economies that allows them to retain their aboriginal methods of obtaining foods and at the same time satisfy the wants that have been created by contact with the outside world (VanStone, 1960, p. 190).

In southwestern Alaska the continuity between past and present is more noticeable. The people of this area, although affected to some extent by the postwar construction boom, have remained closely connected to the trapping-trading economy and the seasonal commercial fishery. At the same time, they have been aided in achieving cultural stability by the predictable seasonal runs of salmon on which they still depend for most of their food supply. Paralleling the development of wage economy in the north has been the increasing participation of the Eskimos of southwestern Alaska in the commercial fishery. Commercial fishing also takes place during a time of the year that does not interfere with traditional subsistence activities, since subsistence fishing can be carried out at the same time as the commercial variety or later. It is likely that the people of the Kuskokwim River region have adjusted successfully to the new conditions because their involvement in the commercial fishery has been marginal until fairly recently. On the Nushagak, however, there has been more disruption. Changes in the settlement pattern near the close of the nineteenth century, as well as a more recent depletion of the fur and game resources have almost eliminated the aboriginal subsistence pattern. Increasing involvement in the commercial fishery has caused the people of this area to depend on their cash income earned during the summer, and a certain amount of subsistence fishing, to support themselves for the entire year. Thus both diversified hunting and trapping have suffered a marked decline.

In both areas the Eskimos are heavily dependent on economic conditions that show little indication of long-range stability. The northern Eskimos, however, would seem to be in a better position because of their continued strong commitment to traditional subsistence activities. In southwestern Alaska, and particularly in the region of this study, the Eskimos' increasing dependency on income earned through participation in the commercial fishery could lead in time to the same sort of insecurity that has been associated with a trapping-trading economy throughout the North American Arctic and sub-Arctic.

Bibliography

Abercrombie, W. R.
    1900   *Supplementary Expedition into the Copper River Valley, Alaska.* In: Compilation of narratives of exploration in Alaska. Washington.
Alaska Russian church archives, accession 12,766. Vital statistics, Nushagak, 1842-1931. The Library of Congress, Washington.
Anonymous
    1913   Report on the fisheries of Alaska for 1912. *Pacific Fisherman,* vol. 11, no. 1.
Anonymous
    1920a Dr. Joseph Herman Romig. *The Pathfinder,* vol. 1, no. 7.
Anonymous
    1920b New orphanage at Dillingham. *The Pathfinder,* vol. 1, no. 11.
Anonymous
    1921   Unknown portions of the Territory of Alaska. *The Pathfinder of Alaska,* vol. 2, no. 10.
Anonymous
    1941   From Ketchikan to Barrow. *The Alaska Sportsman,* vol. VII, no. 3.
Anonymous
    1947   From Ketchikan to Barrow. *The Alaska Sportsman,* vol. XIII, no. 4.
Anonymous
    1948   Libby cannery uses all-native crew. *Pacific Fisherman,* vol. 46, no. 1.
Anonymous
    1959   Nushagak area in Bristol Bay. *Alaska Call,* vol. 1, no. 3.
Anonymous
    1960   Bristol Bay salmon packs (statistical table). *Pacific Fisherman Yearbook Number,* vol. 58, no. 2.

Anonymous
   1961   Eskimo gillnetters—A new element in Alaska industrial fishing. *Pacific Fisherman,* vol. 59, no. 12.
Anonymous
   n.d.   *Service. The true measurement of any institution lies in the service it renders.* Published by the Alaska Packers Association. n.p.
Bailey, G. W.
   1880   *Report upon Alaska and its people.* The United States Senate, 46th Congress, 2nd session, document 132. Washington.
Baker, M.
   1902   Geographic dictionary of Alaska. United States Geological Survey, bulletin 187. Washington.
Bancroft, H. H.
   1886   *Alaska 1730-1885.* San Francisco.
Barsukov, I. (ed.)
   1886-   *Tvoreniĭa Innokentiĭa Mitropolita Moskovskago.* 3 vols. in 2.
   1888   Moscow.
   1897-   *Pisma Innokentiĭa, Mitropolita Moskovskago i Kolomenskago*
   1901   *1828-1878.* 3 vols. St. Petersburg.
Berkh, V. N.
   1823   Puteshestvie uchenika morekhodstva Andreĭa Ustiŭgova, i sluzhiteleĭ Rossiiskoĭ Amerikanskoĭ Kompanii Fedora Kolmakova i Petra Korsanovskago v 1819 godu. *Sĭevernyi Arkhiv,* pt. 4.
Bower, W. T.
   1926   *Alaska fishery and fur-seal industries in 1924.* Report of the United States Commissioner of Fisheries for the Fiscal Year 1925 with Appendices. Washington.
   1938   *Alaska fishery and fur-seal industries in 1935.* Report of the United States Commissioner of Fisheries for the Fiscal Year 1936 with Appendices. Washington.
Brooks, A. H.
   1904   *Placer Mining in Alaska in 1903.* In: Contributions to economic geology, 1903. United States Geological Survey, bulletin 225. Washington.
Browning, L. (ed.)
   1962   Five years of medical observations in the colonies of the Russian-American Company by Staff Physician Romanowsky and Dr. Frankenhauser. pt. 1. *Alaska Medicine,* vol. iv, no. 2.
Bryant, C. and H. H. McIntyre
   1869   *Resources of Alaska.* 41st Congress, 2nd session, Senate executive document no. 32, pp. 1-43. Washington.

Burykin, A. F.
1957   Chetyre plavaniĩa kapitana Khromchenko. *Priroda*, no. 3, pp. 77-80.

Chernenko, M. B.
1956   *Lavrentiĭ Alekseevich Zagoskin. Ocherk zhizni i deĩatelnosti.* In: Zagoskin, L.A., Puteshestviĩa i issledovaniĩa leĭtenanta Lavrentiĩa Zagoskina v russkoĭ Amerike v 1842-1844 gg. Moscow.

Cobb, J. N.
1907   *The fisheries of Alaska in 1906.* Report of the Commissioner of Fisheries for the Fiscal Year 1906 and Special Papers. Washington.
1931   *Pacific salmon fisheries.* Report of the United States Commissioner of Fisheries for the Fiscal Year 1930 with Appendices. Washington.

Conover, P.
1947   The salmon canning industry. *Alaska Life*, vol. x, no. 3.

Cook, J. and J. King
1785   *A voyage to the Pacific Ocean.* 2nd ed., 3 vols. London.

Cooley, R. A.
1963   *Politics and conservation. The decline of the Alaska salmon.* New York.

Dall, W. H.
1870   *Alaska and its resources.* Boston.
1875   *Abstract of population of the native tribes of Alaska.* In: Annual Report of the Commissioner of Indian Affairs to the Secretary of the Interior for the year 1875. Washington.
1877   *On the distribution and nomenclature of the native tribes of Alaska and the adjacent territory.* In: Tribes of the extreme northwest. Contributions to North American ethnology, vol. 1. Washington.

Documents relative to the history of Alaska. Alaska history research
ms   project, 1936-1938. MS in the University of Alaska Library and the Library of Congress.

Elliott, C. P.
1900   *Salmon fishing grounds and canneries.* In: Compilation of narratives of exploration in Alaska. Washington.

Elliott, H. W.
1875   *A report upon the condition of affairs in the territory of Alaska.* Washington.
1886   *Our arctic province. Alaska and the seal islands.* New York.

Fifteenth census of the United States: 1930. Vol. 1, population.
   1931   Number and distribution of inhabitants. Washington.
Freeman, M.
   1908   *Pacific Fisherman map.* Seattle.
Gregory, H. E. and K. Barnes
   1939   *North Pacific fisheries with special reference to Alaska salmon.*
        Studies of the Pacific no. 3. American Council, Institute of
        Pacific Relations. New York.
Hamilton, J. T.
   1890   *The beginnings of the Moravian mission in Alaska.* Bethlehem.
   1892   The Moravian mission in Alaska. *Christian Literature,* vol. 5,
        pp. 351-357.
   1906   *Report of the official visit of Bishop J. Taylor Hamilton to the*
        mission in southern California and Alaska, 1905. Bethlehem.
Hammerich, L. L.
   1958   The western Eskimo dialects. *Proceedings of the Thirty-*
        Second Congress of Americanists, 1956. Copenhagen.
Hawkins, J. E. and E. A. Dougherty
   1958   *The silver fleece. An economic study of the Bristol Bay region.*
        Alaska Rural Development Board. Juneau.
Hodge, F. W. (ed.)
   1912   *Handbook of American Indians north of Mexico.* Bureau of
        American Ethnology, bulletin 30. Washington.
Holmberg, H. J.
   1856-   *Ethnographische skizzen uber die volker des Russischen*
   1863   *Amerika.* 2 vols. Helsingfors.
Hrdlicka, A.
   1944   *Alaska diary.* Lancaster.
Hughes, C. C.
   1965   Under four flags: Recent culture change among the Eskimos.
        Current Anthropology, vol. 6, no. 1.
Jackson, S.
   1886   *Report on education in Alaska.* Washington.
   1897   *Report on introduction of domestic reindeer into Alaska, 1896.*
        Washington.
   1903   *Twelfth annual report on introduction of domestic reindeer*
        into Alaska, 1902. Washington.
   1904   *Thirteenth annual report on introduction of domestic reindeer*
        into Alaska, 1903. Washington.
   1905   *Fourteenth annual report on introduction of domestic reindeer*
        into Alaska, 1904. Washington.
   1906   *Fifteenth annual report on introduction of domestic reindeer*
        into Alaska, 1905. Washington.

Jenness, D.
1962 *Eskimo administration: I. Alaska.* Arctic Institute of North America, technical paper no. 10. Montreal.
Katz, F. J.
1910 *Gold placers of the Mulchatna.* In: Mineral resources of Alaska, report on progress of investigations in 1909. United States Geological Survey, bulletin 442. Washington.
Khromchenko, V. S.
1824 Otryvki iz zhurnala plavaniia g. Khromchenki, v 1822 godu. *Sievernyi Arkhiv,* pts. 10, 11.
Kitchener, L. D.
1954 *Flag over the north. The story of the Northern Commercial Company.* Seattle.
Lantis, M.
1952 Eskimo herdsmen: Introduction of reindeer herding to the natives of Alaska. In: Spicer, E. H. ed., *Human Problems and Technological Change,* chapter 8. New York.
Madson, C.
1922 The Alaska Peninsula and its Resources. *The Pathfinder,* vol. 3, no. 7.
Malach, H.
1950 Pioneer traces Bay towns' ups-downs. *The Forty Ninth Star,* vol. 35, no. 3.
Marsh, M. C. and J. N. Cobb
1911a *The fisheries of Alaska in 1909.* Report of the Commissioner of Fisheries for the Fiscal Year 1909 and Special Papers. Washington.
1911b *The fisheries of Alaska in 1910.* Report of the Commissioner of Fisheries for the Fiscal Year 1910 and Special Papers. Washington.
McDonald, M.
1894 *Report on the salmon fisheries of Alaska.* Bulletin of the United States Fish Commission, vol. XII, for 1892. Washington.
Mertie, J. B.
1938 *The Nushagak district, Alaska.* United States Geological Survey, bulletin 903. Washington.
Moravian Church
1886 *Proceedings of the one hundred and tenth general meeting and ninety-ninth anniversary of the Society of the United Brethren for Propagating the Gospel among the Heathen,* held at Bethlehem, August 26 and 27, 1886. Bethlehem.
1888 *Proceedings of the one hundred and thirteenth general meeting of the Society of the United Brethren for Propagating the*

Gospel among the Heathen, held at Bethlehem, September 28, 1888. Bethlehem.

1891 *Proceedings of the one hundred and sixteenth general meeting of the Society of the United Brethren for Propagating the Gospel among the Heathen,* held at Bethlehem, August 20, 1891. Bethlehem.

1896 *Proceedings of the one hundred and twenty-first general meeting of the Society of the United Brethren for Propagating the Gospel among the Heathen,* held at Bethlehem, August 20, 1896. Bethlehem.

1897 *Proceedings of the one hundred and twenty-second general meeting of the Society of the United Brethren for Propagating the Gospel among the Heathen,* held at Bethlehem, August 26, 1897. Bethlehem.

1898 *Proceedings of the one hundred and twenty-third general meeting of the Society of the United Brethren for Propagating the Gospel among the Heathen,* held at Bethlehem, August 25, 1898. Bethlehem.

1899 *Proceedings of the one hundred and twenty-fourth general meeting of the Society of the United Brethren for Propagating the Gospel among the Heathen,* held at Bethlehem, August 31, 1899. Bethlehem.

1900 *Proceedings of the Society of the United Brethren for Propagating the Gospel among the Heathen,* for the year ending November 14, 1900. Bethlehem.

1904 *Proceedings of the Society of the United Brethren for Propagating the Gospel among the Heathen,* for the year ending August 25, 1904. Bethlehem.

1906 *Proceedings of the Society of the United Brethren for Propagating the Gospel among the Heathen,* for the year ending August 23, 1906. Annual report of the Foreign Missions of the Moravian Church for the year 1905. Bethlehem.

Moravian Church Archives, Bethlehem, Pennsylvania

ms   *Alaska material, box V, letters, box II, folder 1, no. 5.* Supplement to Levering, J.M. to Bro. Stecker. Bethlehem, October 25, 1905.

ms   *Alaska material, box VI, records of ecclesiastical acts, no. 3.* Carmel mission station: records of baptism, receptions, marriages, deaths, list of members dropped, list of children. 1888-1902.

ms   *Alaska records 1892-1938.* Extracts from the diary of the Moravian mission at Carmel from 1895-1896.

ms   *Kilbuck papers, box 7, folder 1, no. 6.* Notes on the history of the Kuskokwim River, by J. H. Kilbuck.

Moser, J. F.
1899 *The salmon and salmon fisheries of Alaska.* Bulletin of the United States Fish Commission, vol. XVIII, for 1898. Washington.
1902 *The salmon and salmon fisheries of Alaska. Report of the Alaska salmon investigations of the United States Fish Commission steamer Albatross in 1900 and 1901.* Washington.

Nelson, E. W
1899 *The Eskimo about Bering Strait.* Eighteenth Annual Report of the Bureau of American Ethnology, pt. I. Washington.

Nelson, M. L. and D. L. Siedelman
n.d.   *Subsistence fishing in the Nushagak and Togiak districts of Bristol Gay, 1963-1965.* Alaska Department of Fish and Game, Division of Commercial Fisheries, Dillingham, Alaska (interoffice memo).

Norton, R.
1911 The four weeks city of Alaska. *Alaska-Yukon Magazine,* vol. II, no. 1. Seattle.

Osgood, W. H.
1904 *A biological reconnaissance of the base of the Alaska Peninsula.* United States Department of Agriculture. Division of Biological Survey. North American fauna, no. 24. Washington.

Oswalt, W. H.
1963 *Mission of change in Alaska. Eskimos and Moravians on the Kuskokwim.* San Marino.

Oswalt, W. H.
1967 *The Alaskan Eskimos.* San Francisco (in press).

Oswalt, W. H. and J. W. VanStone
1967 *The Ethno-archaeology of Crow Village, Alaska.* Bureau of American Ethnology, bulletin 199, Washington.

Pacific Fisherman, vol. X, no. 7, pp. 12, 16. (Statement about the
1912   employment of native peoples in the Bristol Bay cannieries.)

Petroff, I.
1884 *Report of the population, industries and resources of Alaska.* Washington.
1891 Geographical and ethnological notes on Alaska. *Transactions and Proceedings of the Geographical Society of the Pacific,* vol. II, no. I.

Porter, R. P.
1893 *Report on population and resources of Alaska at the eleventh census: 1890.* Washington.

Roberts, R.
  1940   Shall we ban states fishermen? *Alaska Life,* vol. 3, no. 7.
Rogers, G. W.
  1955   *Preliminary economic survey of Dillingham, Alaska and the*
         Bristol Bay region. Alaska Rural Development Board. Juneau.
Russian-American Company Records
  ms   Communications received, vol. 6, no. 346, folio 102.
  ms   Communications sent, vol. 3, no. 164, folio 270.
                              vol. 6, no. 114, folio 82.
                              vol. 6, no. 244, folios 478, 482.
                              vol. 7, no. 257, folios 269-272.
                              vol. 8, no. 322, folio 247.
                              vol. 9, no. 318, folio 478.
                              vol. 9, no. 321, folios 482-487.
                              vol. 9, no. 460, folios 345-349.
                              vol. 9, no. 555, folio 444.
                              vol. 11, no. 73, folios 95-97.
                              vol. 11, no. 272, folio 252.
                              vol. 12, no. 356, folios 152-153.
                              vol. 14, no. 244, folios 274-275.
                              vol. 15, no. 244, folios 314-315.
                          *   vol. 16, no. 466, folios 176-177.
                              vol. 16, no. 467, folios 178-179.
                              vol. 16, no. 479, folios 187-189.
                              vol. 17, no. 387, folios 370-371.
                              vol. 17, no. 388, folios 371-372.
                              vol. 17, no. 444, folios 425.
                              vol. 17, no. 509, folios 493-497.
                              vol. 18, no. 335, folios 314-317.
                              vol. 19, no. 147, folios 186-187.
                              vol. 20, no. 43, folios 51-56.
                              vol. 21, no. 38, folio 25.
                              vol. 21, no. 30, folio 27.
                              vol. 21, no. 35, folios 31-32.
                              vol. 23, no. 703, folio 554.
                              vol. 26, no. 488, folios 381-382.
                              vol. 27, no. 267, folios 386-387.
                              vol. 27, no. 325, folio 463.
                              vol. 32, no. 278, folios 132-133.
                              vol. 34, no. 382, folio 130.
                              vol. 38, no. 115, folio 29.

vol. 38, no. 266, folio 79.
vol. 42, no. 53, folio 138.
vol. 42, no. 445, folio 166.
vol. 47, no. 127, folio 42.

Schanz, A. B.
1891   Our Alaska expedition. *Frank Leslie's Illustrated Newspaper*, vol. LXXII, no. 1881, pp. 138-139, no. 1882, p. 156.

Schwalbe, A. B.
1951   *Dayspring on the Kuskokwim. The story of Moravian missions in Alaska*. Bethlehem.

Shawhan, J. M.
1902   Christmas in southwestern Alaska. *Overland Monthly*, vol. 40, pp. 510-516.

Smith, P. S.
1917   *The Lake Clark-central Kuskokwim region, Alaska*. United States Geological Survey, Bulletin 655. Washington.

Spurr, J. E.
1900   *A reconnaissance in southwestern Alaska in 1898*. Twentieth Annual Report of the United States Geological Survey, 1898-99, pt. 4, Explorations in Alaska in 1898. Washington.

Styles, B.
1910   Developing another portion of the mineral empire of Alaska (Nushagak and Mulchatna river valleys). *Alaska-Yukon magazine*, vol. 10, pp. 132-133.

Swanton, J. R.
1952   *The Indian tribes of North America*. Bureau of American Ethnology, bulletin 145. Washington.

Swineford, A. P.
1898   *Alaska, its history, climate and natural resources*. Chicago and New York.

Tanner, Z. L.
1891   *The fishing grounds of Bristol Bay, Alaska: a preliminary report upon the investigations of the United States Fish Commission steamer Albatross during the summer of 1890*. United States Fish and Wildlife Service, bulletin of the United States Fish Commission, 1889, vol. 9. Washington.

1893   *Report upon the investigations of the United States Fish Commission Steamer Albatross from July 1, 1889 to June 30, 1891*. United States Commission of Fish and Fisheries. Report of the commissioner for 1889 to 1891. Washington.

Tebenkov, M. D.
  1852 *Atlas sieverozapadnykh beregov Ameriki ot Beringova proliva
         do mysa Korrientes i ostrovov Aleutskikh c prisovokupleniem
         niekotorykh miest Sieverovostochnago berega Azii. Gidro-
         graficheskiia zamiechaniia k atlasu sieverozapadnykh beregov
         Ameriki, ostrovov Aleutskikh i niekotorykh drugikh miest
         Sievernago Tikhogo okeana.* St. Petersburg.

Tikhmenev, P. A.
  1939- *The historical review of the formation of the Russian-Ameri-*
  1940   *can Company and its activity up to the present time.* 2 pts.
         St. Petersburg. (Translated by Dimitri Krenov, Works Prog-
         ress Administration, Seattle, Washington, 1939-1940.)

Townsend, J. B.
  n.d.   *Ethnohistory and culture change of the Pedro Bay Tanaina.*
         Unpublished Ph.D. thesis, University of California, Los An-
         geles.

Townsend, J. B. and S-J.
  1961 Archaeological investigations at Pedro Bay, Alaska. *Anthro-
         pological Papers of the University of Alaska,* vol. 10, no. 1,
         pp. 25-58.

*United States census of population 1960, Alaska, number of inhabi-
tants.*
  1960 Final report PC (1) 3A, United States Department of Com-
         merce, Bureau of the Census, Washington.

United States Department of the Interior. Annual Report of the Commissioner of Education.
  1889 *Report of the Commissioner of Education for the year 1887-
         1888.* Washington.
  1891 *Report of the Commissioner of Education for the year 1888-
         1889,* vol. 2. Washington.
  1894 *Report of the Commissioner of Education for the year 1890-
         1891,* vol. 2. Washington.
  1896 *Report of the Commissioner of Education for the year 1894-
         1895,* vol. 2. Washington.
  1897 *Report of the Commissioner of Education for the year 1895-
         1896,* vol. 2. Washington
  1900 *Report of the Commissioner of Education for the year 1898-
         1899,* vol. 2. Washington.
  1902 *Report of the Commissioner of Education,* vol. 2. Washing-
         ton.
  1903 *Report of the Commissioner of Education for the year 1902,*
         vol. 2. Washington.

1905 Report of the Commissioner of Education for the year 1903, vol. 2. Washington.

1907 Report of the Commissioner of Education for the year ending June 30, 1906, vol. 1. Washington.

1908 Report of the Commissioner of Education for the year ending June 30, 1907, vol. 1. Washington.

1909 Report of the Commissioner of Education for the year ending June 30, 1908, vol. 2. Washington.

1910 Report of the Commissioner of Education for the year ended June 30, 1909, vol. 2. Washington.

1911 Report of the Commissioner of Education for the year ended June 30, 1910, vol. 2. Washington.

1912 Report of the Commissioner of Education for the year ended June 30, 1911, vol. 2. Washington.

1918 Report of the Commissioner of Education for the year ended June 30, 1918. Washington.

United States Department of the Interior. Annual Report of the Governor of Alaska.

1887 Report of the Governor of Alaska for the fiscal year 1887. Washington.

1891 Report of the Governor of Alaska for the fiscal year 1891. Washington.

1895 Report of the Governor of Alaska to the Secretary of the Interior, 1895. Washington.

1898 Report of the Governor of the district of Alaska to the Secretary of the Interior, 1898. Washington.

1899 Report of the Governor of the district of Alaska to the Secretary of the Interior, 1899. Washington.

1908 Report of the Governor of the district of Alaska to the Secretary of the Interior, 1908. Washington.

1914 Report of the Governor of Alaska to the Secretary of the Interior, 1914. Washington.

1915 Report of the Governor of Alaska to the Secretary of the Interior, 1915. Washington.

1916 Report of the Governor of Alaska to the Secretary of the Interior, 1916. Washington.

1920 Report of the Governor of Alaska to the Secretary of the Interior, 1920. Washington.

1922 Report of the Governor of Alaska to the Secretary of the Interior, 1922. Washington.

1923 Report of the Governor of Alaska to the Secretary of the Interior, 1923. Washington.

1925   *Report of the Governor of Alaska to the Secretary of the Interior, 1925.* Washington.

1926   *Report of the Governor of Alaska to the Secretary of the Interior, 1926.* Washington.

1931   *Annual report of the Governor of Alaska to the Secretary of the Interior, 1931.* Washington.

1932   *Annual report of the Governor of Alaska to the Secretary of the Interior for the fiscal year ended June 30, 1932.* Washington.

1939   *Annual report of the Governor of Alaska to the Secretary of the Interior for the fiscal year ended June, 30, 1939.* Washington.

n.d.   *Annual report of the Governor of Alaska to the Secretary of the Interior, fiscal year ended June 30, 1946.* Washington.

1952   *Annual report of the Governor of Alaska to the Secretary of the Interior, fiscal year ended June 30, 1952.* Washington.

United States Department of the Interior. Annual Report of the Secretary of the Interior.

1940   *Annual report of the Secretary of the Interior for the fiscal year ended June 30, 1940.* Washington.

1949   *Annual report of the Secretary of the Interior, fiscal year ended June 30, 1949.* Washington.

VanStone, J. W.

1958   Commercial whaling in the Arctic Ocean. *Pacific Northwest Quarterly,* vol. 49, no. 1.

1959   Russian exploration in interior Alaska. An extract from the journal of Andrei Glazunov. *Pacific Northwest Quarterly,* vol. 50, no. 2.

1960   A successful combination of subsistence and wage economies at the village level. *Economic Development and Cultural Change,* vol. VIII, no. 2.

1962a   Notes on nineteenth century trade in the Kotzebue Sound area, Alaska. *Arctic Anthropology,* vol. 1, no. 1.

1962b   *Point Hope, an Eskimo village in transition.* Seattle.

1964   Some aspects of religious change among native inhabitants of west Alaska and the Northwest Territories. *Arctic Anthropology,* vol. 2, no. 2.

n.d.   *Tikchik village, a nineteenth century riverine community in southwestern Alaska* (unpublished manuscript).

White, J. W.

1869   *A cruise in Alaska.* 40th Congress, 3rd session, Senate executive doc. no. 8, pp. 1-10. Washington.

Wrangell, F. P.
1839a Obitateli severo-zapadnikh beregov Ameriki. *Syn Otechestva,* vol. 7, pp. 51-82.
1839b *Statitische und ethnographische nachrichten uber die Russischen besitzungen an der Nordwestkuste von Amerika.* In: Bietrage zur Kenntniss des Russischen Reiches und der angranzenden Lander Asiens, bd. 1. St. Petersburg.
Zagoskin, L. A.
1956 *Puteshestviĩa i issledovaniĩa leĩtenanta Lavrentiĩa Zagoskina v russkoĩ Amerike v 1842-1844 gg.* Moscow.

Index

Index

Nushagak Packing Company, 151
Nushagak River: description of, xvii-
xviii; exploration of, 3-20 *passim;*
and plundering of villages, 4; settlements on, 114, 115
Nushagak village site, xvi
Nuyakuk River, xv, 143, 144; navigation of, xvii; description of,
xviii-xix; animals of, xx; explorations of, 9, 10, 18; on maps, 12,
13; *odinochka* on, 52; and Nushagagmiut, 111; settlements on, 114,
115; and caribou, 132; and trapping, 136

Ogulmiut, 111
Ohogamiut, 4
Old Koliganek, 18, 115, 144, 145,
149
Old Stuyahok, 116, 117, 147. *See
also* Stuyahok
Oriental laborers, 46, 116. *See also*
Chinese
Orlov, Vasili E., 33-34, 36, 37, 40,
90, 91, 92
Orphanages, 104, 120
Orthodox Church. *See* Russian Ortho-
dox Church
Osgood, Wilfred H.: quoted, 14,
101; explorations of, 17-18, 60
Otter, xx, 7, 50, 51, 53, 58, 59, 60,
127, 134

Pacific American Fisheries cannery,
80, 139, 153
Pacific Packing and Navigation
Company, 70
Pacific Steam Whaling Company, 70
Paimiut, xx
Patykov, Gavril, 5
Paugvik, 48
Petelin, Ilia: at Nushagak and
Kuskokwim, 25-26; at Kodiak, 28
Petroff, Ivan: and census, 15; quoted
on Eskimos and Christianity, 35-
36; quoted on salmon, 67; and
population groupings, 111; and
estimate of population, 113, 116;
quoted on immigrants to Nushagak, 119-20; quoted on transportation, 122; quoted on houses,
124-25; quoted on firearms, 127

Philaret, Metropolitan of Moscow,
28, 29, 90
Picnic Point, xv
Pike fishing, 135
Platinum, 147
Point Barrow, xxii, 142
Point Hope, xxii, 80; and reindeer
herding, 163; and education, 164
Point Protection, 127
Poplar tres, xviii, xix
Population, viii; of Aglegmiut and
Kiatagmiut, xxi; of Alexandrovski,
5-6; of Christians at Nushagak,
25, 29, 34; of Kokwok, 47; re-
distribution of, 48; estimates of
Nushagak River region discussed,
111-14, 115; of salmon canning
industry, 116; of Wood River and
Mulchatna, 117; movements of,
118-21; of Koliganek, 144; of
Ekwok, 149-50; of Portage Creek,
150; of Clark's Point, 151; of
Ekuk, 152; of Dillingham and
Kanakanak, 155; of Lake Alek-
nagik, 156; shifts in, 161-62
Porcupine, xx
Portage Creek, xviii, 131, 137, 145;
and tides, xv; school at, 98; and
medical facilities, 105; village
history of, 150
Porter, R. P., 74
Port Moller, xxi
Precipitation: discussed, xix
Prehistory: of Nushagak area, xxiii,
xxiv. *See also* Archaeological sites
Pribilof Islands, 22, 59
Pricing: of fish, discussed, 80-81
Prince William Sound, xx, xxii, 55,
57
*Proceedings of the Society of the
United Brethren for Propagating
the Gospel among the Heathen,*
17n
Prospecting, 14, 17, 61. *See also*
Mining
Ptarmigan, xx, 135
Pulmonary diseases: epidemic of
1886, 101. *See also* Tuberculosis
Purchase: of Alaska, 13, 33, 110, 160

Quinhagak, 47

Racks: for fish, described, 138